River of Promise

River of Promise

Two Women's Story of Love and Adoption

written by
Judy Dahl

San Diego, California

LuraMedia

© Copyright 1989 LuraMedia
San Diego, California
International Copyright Secured
Publisher's Catalog Number LM-614
Printed and Bound in the United States of America

LuraMedia
7060 Miramar Road, Suite 104
San Diego, CA 92121

All Scripture quotations unless otherwise noted are from the Revised Standard Version of the Holy Bible, copyright 1946, 1952, 1971 by the Division of Christian Education, National Council of the Churches of Christ in the U.S.A. Used by permission.

9-89

Library of Congress Cataloging-in-Publication Data
Dahl, Judy, 1948.
    River of promise : two women's story of love and adoption / by Judy Dahl
    p.   cm.
    ISBN 0-931055-64-4
    1. Lesbian mothers—United States—Case studies.   2. Adoption—United States—
Case Studies   I. Title.
HQ75.53.D35   1989
306.8'74—dc19   88-32229
                                                                               CIP

Book

Dedicated to

―――――――――――――――――――――――

Terryl, the love of my life and life partner,
Noah, who gave us our first glimpse of the rainbow,
Andy and Jori, the children who came to us from the river,
and Gracie,
the Mother of us all.

―――――――――――――――――――――――

Acknowledgements

This book has been written because of the original nudge of Adam Geiger, given to his mother, Lura, who sensed that I might have a story. It is also because of the persistent love and encouragement of my many friends and my dear family that I believed in myself enough to begin this work.

I would like to extend special thanks to my pastor and friend, Nancy Wilson, who took time out of her busy schedule to review this work; to my friend Joy Alesdatter, whose technical ability and original gift enabled me to begin writing; to Nancy Hardesty, my editor; to Carol Jeanotilla, my friend of many years who illustrated this work; Rhea Miller, who first showed me the river; and to Terryl, who walked each step with me.

Judy Dahl
1988

Contents

the window

Looking through the nursery window that early October morning, I see the past years of our river journey being replayed.

It feels almost numbing to finally be here, looking in on your small, tender life, a life which will mold and transform me in ways I do not even know.

I give you permission to touch me, cause me to weep, to love, and to delight as I have with no other. I offer you my life, unbounded. I will be your mother. Your mother? Having never been a mother before, this could be quite a kick for both of us. Have you chosen me? Are we truly beginning a journey beyond our independent lives? Will you trust me with your young life? I haven't been around very many little boys before. You're so small. You are so purple when you cry. I wish you wouldn't cry so hard. I wish I could hold you. I want to feel you soft and warm beside me.

Gracie, I'm terrified — scared to death that I won't know what to do with this child. I want to thank you, thank you so much for this little baby. I've waited so long for this moment, and now here I am acting weird. But it feels weird! All of a sudden I'm a mother, and I don't even know what that means. Please help me. You know what it is to be a mother. You have mothered me all my life. You have held me warm and close and cuddled me in your warm, soft arms. Give me your mother's heart. I know we can do this together. Help me, help us.

1

Terryl stood there looking in the same window.

"Honey, what do you think?"

I ask her first because I'm so afraid to put my feelings out there where the air can touch them. I'm afraid I won't say it right, or do it right, or be right. I so want to do this right. I want to be a good parent. No, I want to be a great parent. The best! "There's no sense doing something if you're not going to do it right." I hear my mother repeating this in my mind as she did so often when I was a child.

"I think he's absolutely beautiful! What shall we name him?"

See, she's all ready to name him, and I'm not sure I even know this is really happening. Oh God, are we doing the right thing?

Why, Sugar, this is the window you've been looking for. This is the dream you've been chasing down the river. This is where you've taken yourself. I've been with you every step of the way. I'm not going anywhere now. You just keep believing in yourself. Don't be afraid.

"Isn't he the most precious child you've ever seen? What shall we name him?"

Having dogeared every baby name book that jumped out at us in the bookstores, we have somehow managed to come down to two boys' names.

"I think we need to hold him and talk to him about his name before we make it final."

This must be the eighties. I don't remember anybody asking me what name I wanted. The most up-to-date literature now suggests, however, that the baby be included in the naming experience. It does make some sense. We decided to wait and name him when we can hold him.

The nurse was suctioning him out and cleaning him up a little, washing the river journey from his young body.

"Nurse, can we hold our son?"

"Your son? I'm afraid there must be some mistake. This child belongs to Susan Munez. She's just coming out of surgery."

* * *

The arrangement had been that Mrs. Munez would call us when Susan went into labor. Every time the phone rang our hearts went flying out of our months as we ran, winded, to answer. This labor and birth called up from us feelings we never knew we had.

The call came minutes after Susan had been taken to the hospital. I was in the kitchen cooking supper, caught off guard in one of those rare moments when I was not connecting the ringing phone to the labor room. Isn't that the way it goes? "A watched baby never labors," or something like that. We had made some intentional decisions to back off from hysteria since Susan was now almost two weeks past her due date. So there I was, steaming vegetables, humming a lullaby, imagining the phone to be another curious friend anxious to hear some baby news.

"Hello."

"Susan just went into labor."

The next thing I knew the vegetables were off the stove and I was flying up the stairs to launch our suitcase over the bannister. I made airline reservations and then called Terryl to meet me at the airport. I sped down the Coast Highway and panted up to the ticket counter. I told the agent our entire story while she prepared our tickets. I spotted Terryl running toward me just as I started for the departure gate.

After take off — this time in the plane — we reminded each other to give thanks for this high moment in our lives, a moment we'd waited for for so many years, years of looking up the river, waiting, longing, believing. We held hands, and I remember seeing God in my mind . . .

Gracie, here we are! It really is happening. You really did come through for us, you really did. You truly are the God of all creation.

She looked at me as she had so many other times when I dreamed of a child in my prayers. There she was with a face as big as a picture screen and a warm tender smile. As always she was wearing her huge colorful skirt filled with pockets where she keeps blessings and answers to dreams. In my prayer that evening she began to reach deep inside a pocket, smiling.

I imagined myself taking Terryl to rest in her lap, finding a place for our joy and some respite from our hysteria, a quiet place to relax near the end of a long river journey.

"What are you thinking about?"

Terryl almost always knew when Gracie and I were spending time together.

"God is smiling with us, Honey."

* * *

3

Mrs. Munez picked us up at the airport and hurried us off to the hospital. We had rushed so during the past few hours that by the time we reached the hospital, we were jogging up and down the aisles.

Others in the waiting room were curious. Two women had just flown in but had not yet landed. Eventually our pace settled, and we joined the ranks of expectant parents, sharing the footpath worn by the many before us.

We heard the stories of Susan's birth. This occasion was taking Mrs. Munez back. We heard the similarities and differences between Susan's and Mrs. Munez's own birth from Great-Grandmother. We carefully stored all of this information to share later with our child. We spoke with tenderness for each other and shared dreams for the future. We continued to weave the fabric of the blended family we'd begun months before, the color and texture deepening as we labored. Close to midnight we began to realize our human needs once again.

"I'm hungry."

I almost wished I hadn't said anything. Out came the picnic basket the pending Grandmother had packed for the occasion. In short order the waiting room turned into a deli — a last supper before the birth.

When will this labor end? Gracie, keep them safe, please.

It's okay, Sugar.

She calls me "Sugar," especially when I'm frightened. God gives me the information I need, just before I need it, rarely one second earlier. That night I was listening closely, trying to hear above the roar in my head, straining for any morsel of input from Gracie. She was mostly silent, smiling.

We closed down the deli about two in the morning. The other families in the waiting room had gathered at our table. Anxiety makes one very hungry, and food is such an equalizer. Terryl and I continued to place our footprints in the worn linoleum.

Susan's birthing coach joined us in the waiting room, this time to tell us that the doctor had decided to do a Caesarean section.

I said all my prayers at once: "Hail Mary. . .Glory be. . .Our Gracie. . ."

The swinging doors hit the wall the same way they had for other babies that night. This time we knew the opening doors were ours. The doctor flew by us in his greens, and there in the crook of his arm was a mouth wailing at the world, a little blue baby.

"Is that one ours. . .ours. . .?"

4

The no-longer-pending-but-now-actual Grandmother, Great-Grandmother, labor coach, Terryl, and I all smushed our faces against the nursery window.

The nurse held him up to the glass.

Is that the nurse, or is it you, Gracie?

But God remembered Noah and all the beasts and all the cattle that were with him in the ark. And God made a wind blow over the earth, and the waters subsided; the fountains of the deep and the windows of the heavens were closed, the rain from the heavens was restrained, and the waters receded from the earth continually. At the end of a hundred and fifty days the waters had abated; and in the seventh month, on the seventeenth day of the month, the ark came to rest upon the mountains of Ar'arat. . . . At the end of forty days Noah opened the window of the ark which he had made. . . (Gen. 8:1-4, 6).

The river trip was ending.

Gracie
the God of my creation

Sometimes, at what seems the end of a long journey, you begin to realize that making dreams takes a lot out of you. Fortunately for dream makers, it gives a lot in return.

Ten years before finding myself at the nursery window, I spotted someone coming up the river who opened my eyes and my heart like a tree reaching out for rain in the midst of summer. I can remember every detail of our first meeting. I especially remember the silence which came when nothing else filled the space between us. Somehow, I knew this person from the images that filled my mind when I was a small child. My mother always told me, "Someday you'll find someone just like Daddy to spend your life with." She sure didn't look like Daddy, but for the first time ever I knew what my mother meant.

We met when both our lives were filled with other lovers, a budding career for Terryl, and a changing career for me.

Terryl grew up in a large Roman Catholic family with five other children who have always meant the world to her. She was second in birth order, the first girl. She lived all her formative years in Denver, Colorado, the third generation in a prominent family. Terryl had a special connection to her Grammy. Always very popular at her parochial school, she completed her senior year as student body president.

After graduation, Terryl began college at the San Francisco College for Women. She ultimately received a bachelor's degree in journalism and later a master's degree from the University of Colorado. She taught English in a Denver middle school and eventually struck out on her own — after a four-month solo tour of Europe — for Tucson, Arizona. She had lived there only a few months when a major tragedy struck her family. Her mother became desperately ill. Terryl went home. Just a few days later her mother died. Terryl was left with an intense desire to stay close to her father, her sisters, and her two brothers. She did not return to Tucson until many years later.

Terryl began then to build her career in Denver as an administrator of social service programs. She put her heart, broken from the death of her mother, into her work and into healing and building with her family. She became very successful and eventually founded an agency which helped delinquent young people rebuild their lives. It was at this place in the river that I met Terryl.

I, too, was coming up the river from a full and varied life. I was the first of the last-born in my family, which is to say I am the first-born of identical twins. I shared my very early life with a brother twelve years older than me whom I remember with deep love. I cherish memories of one who teased me and wouldn't let us watch "Howdy Doody" so he could see Eddie Fisher on the then-novel televison set every evening. He was married and having children before I finished the fourth grade. My older sister was only four years ahead of us, so we shared lots of childhood rituals: getting carsick in the backseat when Daddy refused to stop during those interminably long summer vacation drives, heated debates over who would wash and who would dry the dishes.

Being a twin was a very mixed bag. Sibling rivalry is heightened to an incredible extent for twins, at least it was for this twin. Jan and I were close playmates and friends some of the time, but over the years we chose different friends and our lives took very different courses. We fought for attention and position and played a seemingly endless game of trying to find our own individual space in this world of twins. We won a twin contest as children. We dressed alike and looked so much alike that people called us "Twin" rather than using our names because they couldn't tell us apart. I rebelled at that and wanted desperately to be an individual.

8

We all went to Roman Catholic schools through high school. I always had a crush on one or another of the nuns. Once I reached sixth grade my favorite nun became the same one for many years, and I followed her into the convent immediately after high school.

I remember the night I told my father of my decision. "Daddy, I have a vocation, and I want your permission to enter the convent."

"It's a tough life, Judy," he said. We never talked about it again. I had already told my mother who, as much as I think she grieved over it herself, agreed to support my decision. My mother was a Methodist, and while she didn't quite understand the need for a young woman to enter a convent, she was always open to the religion of my father.

Looking back on this now, I realize that I may have subconsciously seen entering religious life as my ticket to independence. I remember thinking I wanted to "save the world," but had I been even slightly astute at the time, I would have seen how very difficult that is to do when one is cloistered from the world!

Up until that point in my life, I had lived a rather happy, well-protected, and loved existence. My father and mother loved each other, and we always knew they loved us. Daddy worked hard, and Mother was home working hard with us throughout our growing up years. I never remember a night without a home-cooked meal. My memories of childhood are filled with laughter, family, friends, and goodness. I was very blessed.

I entered a Benedictine convent in Duluth, Minnesota, a far cry from everything I had known in Phoenix. I almost got frostbite on my toes the first winter, and I took a few emotional falls as well. I had a variety of deep, intense feelings for other sisters and spent a lot of energy trying to be good and follow the rules. I worked hard at not having any "special friendships."

I had no sense of myself as a sexual person at this point. I had dated one or two boys in high school and had always managed to find a date for the prom, but I was much more interested in going to school on Saturday afternoons to help the nuns clean their rooms. I always thought that was because God wanted me to be a nun. I was lonely during those Duluth days. I missed my family and the warmth of the sun, but I stayed, thinking I was doing what I should.

Not long after I received the habit and became Sister Judith, I began to wonder how much longer I could stay. I struggled with the decision and finally left one very cold, bleak January day.

It took me some time to rally, but a few months after I returned to Phoenix, I applied to become a flight attendant with a Denver-based airline. On my first flight out, the lead flight attendant introduced me as the flying nun. During the next eleven years, I flew and went to school and fell in love for the first time. I fell in love with the supervisor of flight attendant training — a woman. The feelings were so strong and the experience so intense, it took me years after that to come to terms with myself. The raft in the river dipped and tipped, and I went overboard several times.

I spent the next six or seven years wrestling with God over my heart. It was a long, painful process to reconcile my spirituality and my sexuality. I had always heard that to be a lesbian was an abomination to God and an aberration. Yet I knew in my heart that it was as much a part of who I was as the color of my eyes. After much thought and prayer, I decided that I would do the very hardest thing I could think of to get back into God's good graces. From what I had heard, adopting a Mormon lifestyle should do it. So I moved to Salt Lake City and became a Mormon, hoping to root this evil from my life. But it didn't work for me. There was no wind in my sails, the river was drying up below me, so I returned to Denver. I continued flying and decided to finish my undergraduate degree in human services. I was required to do an internship, and I chose the agency in which Terryl was executive director.

I walked upstairs to meet her in her office for the interview. As we rounded our individual bends in the river and found one another for the first time, we only stared and smiled. It must have been thirty seconds before we spoke — which normally is not a great deal of time, but it is unusual for a job interview. We wiped the river from our consciousness and unknowingly left the office that day with our rafts connected for a new journey.

I worked with Terryl for only a short time before I hit some more rapids that sent me reeling for a couple of years. She stood beside me through some very rugged times, and we stayed connected through occasional phone calls. Terryl was in a relationship with another woman when we met so we were silent about our feelings, simply sharing warmth and friendship during our brief and infrequent meetings. Sometimes weeks, even months would go by without our seeing one another. Yet at each new meeting we knew our love had grown still deeper. Years passed. Terryl moved on to another social service agency, and her relationship with the other woman changed course. By then I had quit flying and was in my first year of seminary, preparing for the ministry.

The river honored our journey. Four and a half years later, the person I had spotted coming up the river had become ever clearer in my vision. Our rafts had stayed connected.

* * *

I was feeling particularly nervous that Sunday morning before Christmas. I was just completing my first semester of seminary and felt like a novice as I approached the pulpit. I looked into the congregation and thought I would collapse from shock and sheer delight when I spotted Terryl.

The service for me that day was a whirl. I felt like I had earlier that spring, rafting down the Colorado River. I couldn't keep my mouth and stomach together! Afterward Terryl and I went to a restaurant for brunch.

Before that Sunday was over, we both knew that our friendship was growing wings. We had been friends for so many years that we'd talked about children and about our dreams over many lunches. But this wasn't the same kind of sharing we'd done in the past, when we'd guarded our secret. That night a kind of grafting began. Children were no longer distant stories that crept into our list of dreams. They began to take shape and form in our words. We knew then, without speaking, that our words would someday begin to attach themselves to the labor of our love. We were planting the seeds of our family.

From the first silent meeting at the river bend through the four and a half years of rapid lives for both of us, we had always known of our love. The river has a time for everything, and though it seemed sometimes long and impossible for us to gather together at the river, our time had come.

We moved in together several days after that brunch. We prepared our home together and filled it with loving, becoming lovers after years of being friends. In my home, I had kept a small banner that read: "If you love something very very much, let it go free. If it does not return to you, it was never meant to be yours; if it does, love it forever." I had purchased the banner and hung it up in my house shortly after meeting Terryl the first time. We had a special little ceremony as I hung it near the doorway of our first home together.

After a few months, the subject of children made its way into our home. Soon after all the boxes were unpacked, we made an appointment with a noted gynecologist. The visit was more confusing than helpful. There was still so much unknown about donor insemination. Terryl and I also had a great deal to work out before settling on such a big decision. I had two years left to complete my seminary training, and we wanted more time alone as a couple. Finances were tight with only one solid income, and the first two years of adjusting to each other were rugged from time to time. We decided it was too early to begin the process.

We spent the next few years developing our careers. Children were always in our plans. We thought in terms of donor insemination, mostly, I suppose, because some of our close friends were in the process of insemination and it seemed like an eventuality. That is, until the day I was called out of class.

Our friend Rachel had become pregnant with her first insemination. We had all been so thrilled. Now only a month later I rushed to the hospital to sit with her partner Barb during Rachel's surgery. Rachel had an ectopic pregnancy. She lost the fetus and quite a bit of blood. I waited with Barb in the room they had assigned to Rachel after recovery. All she said as they wheeled her into the room was, "Never again!"

Our dreams, too, faded a bit that day.

The class I had left was on pastoral care and counseling, yet I felt so helpless at the hospital. Technique washed away with grief. These women had been talking about having a child for years. What could I give them? What was left? I was numb. Terryl was too. Dinner that night was quiet. I unraveled the baby blanket I had begun to knit for their baby.

Rest your little head right here and be still. Go get Terryl and let me hold the both of you in my arms. I can hold you up. You're not too heavy for me, not even with your wounded dreams. I've got Barb and Rachel in my skirt, too. Rest now. Dare to dream again. I give you my courageous heart. Here. . . take it from my pocket.

After experiencing a wounded dream so close to home, I poured myself into school. As I pondered the ultimate questions — "Who are we? Who is God? Where are we going" — I found God looking very unusual to me. I used to see the old man in the sky. He was always kind enough and good enough to be God. He was protective and eager to help, but he didn't look much like me or my other best friends. There grew a distinct recognition in me that the God I had seen in my prayers for years now looked rather odd.

Some people in seminary and some of those on the fringes of my life were talking a lot those days about "white light." I tried to picture God as white light for awhile, but it nearly blinded me. Besides, it seemed weird to ask white light to put its arms around me. "White light" didn't brighten my world as much as I wanted. For the very first time in my life, I began to understand that being "made in God's image" doesn't just mean that I look like God but also that God looks like me!

In my final year of seminary, I took a course titled "The Preacher and Contemporary Literature." We were asked to read many short stories, novels, poems, and plays. At the end of the the semester, we were told to go through all of the characters in all of the books we had read to find the character that most resembled God to us. The character who most reminded me of God was Mama in Lorraine Hansberry's play <u>A Raisin in the Sun</u>.

Mama is kind and honest. She has an intense loyalty to her children. She respects all living things, her people and her plants. She loves with such depth but puts up with no nonsense. She loves all her kids with a forever heart. She enjoys feeding her family. And she wears this huge skirt and an apron filled with pockets where she stores treasures for everyone. She is a <u>home</u>maker, making a gift of home wherever she is welcome, taking her world and molding and shaping it with love and strength, and out of wisdom and truth creating the best of life. Her faith is in her kids, in her people, and in herself. She is tender and bold. She works hard, plays hard, gives and takes and gathers. She leads and stands firm and dreams big and hopes forever. . .and beyond.

As I worked on that paper for class, I began to develop a relationship with Mama. The first time I went to her in prayer, heaven smelled like Sunday dinner. I thought back then to a time in my childhood home when my mother was fixing chicken and dumplings for a Sunday meal. Ever since that class, I see God becoming in such big and tender ways. She is ever present, all-knowing, and amazing. That's what I know most about her. She <u>is amazing</u>. As my relationship with her grew, I found a new image, a new way of seeing and believing God.

One Sunday not long after this realization came to me, we sang the hymn "Amazing Grace" at the end of the service. My eyes teared. For the first time in my entire life, I felt touched so tenderly by a God who was what I needed and wanted in my life. Today I call her Gracie! I want to tell of her strength, her goodness, her untiring arms. . .Gracie, the God of my creation, who is mother, sister, friend, and amazing!

* * *

The day I was called out of class to meet Barb and Rachel at the hospital, I went to Gracie in prayer.

But, Gracie, the children. . .

When you begin to dream big dreams, there may be days filled only with mourning. Some dreams take great precision and exact timing to make just right. I will hold you until the morning comes again. Now gather up your loved ones and come, rest awhile. There will be other days. . .with the dawn comes rejoicing.

Make yourself an ark of gopher wood; make rooms in the ark, and cover it inside and out with pitch. This is how you are to make it: the length of the ark three hundred cubits, its breadth fifty cubits, and its height thirty cubits. Make a roof for the ark, and finish it to a cubit above; and set the door of the ark in its side; make it with lower, second, and third decks. For behold, I will bring a flood of waters upon the earth, to destroy all flesh in which is the breath of life from under heaven; everything that is on the earth shall die. But I will establish my covenant with you; and you shall come into the ark, you, your sons, your wife, and your sons' wives with you. And of every living thing of all flesh, you shall bring two of every sort into the ark, to keep them alive with you. . .(Gen. 6:14-19).

Gracie reached deep into a pocket and handed us a map.

Time to be moving on. . .

14

the dream

"Honey, can you see Meredith behind us? This snow is pretty thick right in here, and I can hardly see the road. Is she okay?"

"Hmmm, yeah, she's okay. Oh no, she's spinning on the road! Easy, Mer, easy!"

"Should we pull over and help her out?"

"Sure, Honey, and then the three of us can stand in the snow bank over there and heave ho this delicate monster? Sorry, that was pretty nasty. There, she's back on track. I can hardly see through this rear-view mirror, but she looks good."

We were moving from Denver, Terryl's home of thirty-seven years and mine for the past seventeen. Terryl had an especially hard time leaving her family and her roots. But we felt Gracie calling us on to another place in the river. I had been elected to fill a regional position in the Universal Fellowship of Metropolitan Community Churches, the denomination I serve as a clergyperson. It meant I must live in the Los Angeles area.

We loaded up a U-Haul truck and set out, with our friend Meredith driving our car behind us through a treacherous winter storm. As usual, our conversation on this journey called us back to one of our ongoing discussions.

"Now, what were we talking about?"

"Our favorite subject...babies."

"Oh, yeah. Bunkie, do you think this is all just a pipe dream? Are we ever really going to have children, or are we just in love with the idea? One minute I think I want kids, and the next minute I can't figure out where I would fit them into my day. How about you?"

"Well, I'm not sure having children is ever a rational decision. I mean here we are, two very happy people, on our way to California with a very challenging and exciting job waiting for you, and something grand and hidden waiting for me. We have the biggest truck made, filled with our very own stuff."

"Should we have left that extra sofa behind?"

"Well, it's too late now. Anyway, as I was saying, things are going very well for us, and dreams are coming true. We've believed in this moment for a long time."

"And here we are in the middle of the worst ice storm this desert land has ever seen."

"But think of what's beyond. I still want to share our lives with children, don't you?"

"I've always believed we'd have children, and I still do. What do you mean, it's not rational?"

"Well, who in their right mind would choose to bring a person into a life as grand as ours, someone who will keep us up nights, burp on our business suits, and require care for as long as we both shall live? Not to mention worming their way into our golf games and our movie nights?"

"And into our hearts..."

"And that, my friend, is why we're having this discussion."

"You know, every chance I get I ask parents, if they had it to do all over again, would they have children. Not once have I heard anyone say they would change. They all want to tell me how hard it is, and I can see that parenting is a very trying and challenging endeavor..."

"But as hard as it is and as tough as it must be, the world sure isn't hurting for population. Everyone I ask says they wouldn't trade their kids for all the books in the library. They do wish they could read just one book from time to time, however."

"Judy, do you think we would be good parents? What about our baby having two mothers? Now won't that be a trip? Most of us don't know what

16

to do with <u>one</u> mother, and society isn't exactly supportive of us."

"On the other hand, <u>not</u> having children will not endear us to society either."

"That's true. If we waited for others to approve, we'd wait out our lives and die, never having lived at all. Dreams are rarely shared by many. . . at least in the beginning. It's easy to grab onto the tail of a dream and go along after the mountains have been scaled and the rivers forded."

"True, and I care about us, and endearing a child to us and our hearts to a child. I care about our listening to this dream that's been alive and trying to beat its way out of our hearts and into the world for the past several years. We would have so much fun with our kids. I think we'll be good parents."

"This road is getting worse. Go easy. Can you see Meredith?"

"It looks like there's been an accident up ahead. Don't look."

"What do you mean, don't look? I drive better when I look at the road. . . . Now, I see what you mean. I wish I hadn't looked. Say a prayer."

"Can you see Meredith?"

"I've got her in my mirror. She's okay. I wonder if she saw the body. Can you believe it? A dead man in the middle of the freeway, out here in the middle of nowhere? Are you okay, Honey?"

"Yes. I hope it doesn't take long for the ambulance to come. That highway patrol officer looked freaked. It's pretty cold to be standing outside in this beside a dead body."

"If we have a son, he cannot be a police officer."

"Maybe we should let him choose his own career."

"Not on your life. I have every intention of being an overly protective, overbearing mother."

"Terrific! We're off to a rolling start. I think it's a good thing I got to choose my own life's path. . .otherwise, I can assure you, Honey, my momma would not have chosen you for her son-in-law! As much as she loves you, you weren't her first choice!"

"He can't be a police officer, nor will I allow him to ever die on a cold and lonely freeway."

"You know what I think? I think any child in this universe would be terribly lucky to have you for a mother. I know you well enough to know how proud you'd be of our child, no matter what he or she chose to do.

And we shall never let our child die on a cold and lonely freeway. Can we afford this kid who is not allowed to die and whose mother attends all job interviews?"

"I just thought of something. If we're lucky, we will have evolved so much technologically by the time our child is of sound mind and good judgment to choose a career, that police officers will no longer be needed. Instead there will be little robots riding around in saucers to issue tickets to all families with two mothers."

"That's it! No more police officers. Yes, I do want to raise a child. Even a son."

"Providing we have a guarantee there will only be robots."

"Maybe by then we won't have crime, and even robots will be extinct."

"That's good, while we're scheming and dreaming, let's make death extinct too."

"I couldn't bear to lose a child. Maybe we shouldn't have a child, Honey. I just couldn't stand it if we lost our child."

"I know what you mean. I couldn't stand to lose you either. But I wouldn't trade sharing my life with you now for all the books in the library."

"Coming from you, I consider myself loved indeed! Are you ready to give up reading eight different books at once?"

"Only if you and our child are my bookends."

"But can we afford it?"

"If you sell your robot, we can."

"We'll know when the time is right. We'll begin looking into this once we get to California and you get settled in your job and I find one. Money will flow to the right dream. It will happen."

"It looks like the snow has let up. Turn on the radio please, Hon, and let's get a weather update. This static is pretty. . .oh, here goes. . .'with warming temperatures in the Phoenix basin but continuing snow in the northern mountain regions. Phoenix can look forward to some rain showers tonight and possibly tomorrow morning.' "

Gracie, keep us in the river. . .

You're on your way, Sugar. Keep your head up. . .stay close.

Noah did all that [God] had commanded him. . . . And rain fell upon the earth forty days and forty nights (Gen. 7:5, 12).

The map had led us to the river.

the river

Not long after our arrival in California I was asked to bring the message on a Mother's Day. In my sermon I reflected on the journey that had brought me to this place...

"The story just read from the first and second chapters of Exodus takes me back to a Sunday morning many years ago which I would like to share with you in today's message.

"I remember walking into a church that morning, feeling a little uneasy. This was only my second visit to a Metropolitan Community Church — the first time was years earlier — and I wasn't exactly sure how I felt about this church that had a special outreach to gay and lesbian people.

"I was late in arriving, so I quickly took a seat at the back of the church, careful not to lift my eyes until I was seated in the pew. With my composure regained, I looked toward the front, and for the first time in my life, I saw a woman approaching the pulpit. My Roman Catholic heart nearly left my chest.

"She was soft-spoken and gentle, yet her words were marked with passion. She began, 'God is like a river flowing....' She went on to tell the congregation about a recent rafting expedition she had experienced with some of her friends. She'd watched the group just in front of them preparing for their journey and noticed how the children excitedly jumped into the raft while the adults exhibited fear, taking their time getting into the raft.

"Her sermon has never left me. Her presence in church that morning, and her message, are in part responsible for my presence in this pulpit this morning. She took to the river before me. Now living by the ocean myself, I know that God lives there. The ocean is the home where all rivers converge. There is such spirit and such power in water. I've learned new respect for the ocean, and I know a little more about the river. Slowly, I learn more about trust. I've learned to watch the children.

"That river story from so many years ago has led me to the river story which has come to us from the book of Exodus this morning. It has recently flowed into my awareness with intense power.

"This story takes place along the Nile sometime between 1350 and 1200 B.C.E. The children of Israel were in bondage. Among their midwives were Puah and Shiphrah. The new Egyptian Pharaoh felt very threatened by their occupation. They had a great deal of power, being present during the birth of children. Pharaoh could see that the population of the Israelites was expanding, and it scared him to think that their nation might grow larger than his own. So Pharaoh sent word to the midwives that all Jewish boy babies were to be killed at birth and cast into the Nile. Fortunately Shiphrah and Puah refused to obey such a ridiculous rule, and they hid all the little boy babies, sparing their young lives.

"During this time, Jocabed gave birth to a son, Moses. Frightened that the king would find her son and have him killed, she made a basket, waterproofed it as best she could, put her baby boy in the basket, and set it among the reeds at the river's edge.

"The daughter of Pharaoh went to the river to bathe that day and found the basket with the baby boy crying inside. She knew this child was a Hebrew baby, but she had compassion on him.

"Miriam, the sister of Moses, had been watching by the river and saw the daughter of Pharoah find the basket. She rushed to her side and offered to find a Hebrew woman to nurse the child. The princess agreed, and Miriam brought Jocabed to the Pharaoh's daughter for this purpose.

"Can you imagine the courage it took for Jocabed to put her little baby boy into the river? How did she walk away from the river? Trusting God. . .and who else was there? She gave up control, a part of herself, her

20

very flesh and blood, and put it in the river. The system was coming after what she most loved. They wanted to take it from her. . .and she trusted the river.

"Moses came back to her, not just alive, but royal.

"What is it you love most in this world? Will you trust it to the river? Will you trust God? Who else is there for you? How will you build the basket to carry your precious dreams and your most beloved possessions? And then will you have the courage to walk away from the river?

"What we put into the river will come back to us. If we put in anger and resentment, that's what will wash its way up on our shores. If we give love, our hearts, our lives, our dreams to the river, they will come up on the shore of our lives.

"God tells us this story through the life of a mother, through the life of Jocabed. This Mother's Day it is important for us to remember all the deeds of courage, big and small, which our mothers have done for us. It is such a paradox, but sometimes what seems most dangerous might be the very thing to save our lives. Think about how many times our mothers walked away from the river, trusting us to the river. How many times they have learned that God is able to save what they most treasure.

"Let's imagine ourselves going to a river this morning. Standing along the river's edge, let us give some thought to what we will offer to our earthly mothers and to our Heavenly Mother.

"One thing we can be sure of: whatever we offer will return to us again."

* * *

Later, as we settled into the car, I turned to Terryl.

"You know, I learned a lot from my sermon this morning. It's true what they told us in seminary: preachers often speak from the pulpit what they most need to hear themselves. This morning I heard that the time has come to trust our baby dreams to the river. . .to not let the system, the fear of loss keep us from it. When I asked us to consider what we would offer to our mothers, I saw myself placing this great dream in the river. What did you offer, T?"

"I offered love to my mother. I always miss her so much around this time. She died just before Mother's Day thirteen years ago."

"I know, Honey. I wish I could bring her back to you."

"So do I. When I think about having children, I get so terribly sad, knowing that my mother will never see them. Both Mom and Grammy would have been so wonderful with our children, my sisters' and brothers' kids, too. But I really agree with you, Honey. I think today would be a wonderful day to finally give our dream for children to the river."

"Do you think we're ready?"

"Well, Gracie has blessed us both with great jobs, and we've been here long enough to settle in. Maybe it's just because it's Mother's Day, and all these maternal feelings start flowing. But the truth is, we've been talking about this for years now. We've had five years to build our relationship and . . ."

"Yes, let's do it! Where do we begin?"

"I like the idea of having a baby, but the idea of giving birth scares me a little. Maybe we're too old. Why don't we look into both adoption and pregnancy and see which path opens up for us."

"There are so many kids without a home. And very few with two mothers!"

"I'll call around tomorrow and see if I can get us an appointment with an adoption agency."

Gracie, bless the beginning of this journey for us. My offering to you this day as we begin . . .whatever child wants to come and live with us is welcome."

Okay, Sugar. I'm with you all the way.

* * *

"T, I reached the adoption agency, and we have an appointment next Tuesday at four o'clock. Can you make it?"

"I wouldn't miss it for all the books in the library!"

The day of our first appointment was very exciting. We dressed up in our best clothes and bubbled all the way to the agency. We flung open wide the doors on a new beginning . . .

"How are you feeling, Honey?"

"Well, I was feeling terrific, but that woman who just took our names looked at us like we'd just dropped in from outer space. Do you suppose it's the aftereffect of 'two mothers'? But isn't this California . . .'the land of what's happenin' now'. . .land of the free, home of the brave. . .?"

22

"We'll soon find out."

Sugar, just be yourself. Be kind to the people and honest. Let them know how deserving you are of a child.

"Hello, Miss. . .uh, now, which of you is interested in adopting?"

"We both are."

"So, you both want to adopt a separate child?"

"No, we want to adopt one child, together."

"Oh, I see, well, um, now, do you have jobs?"

Is she for real?

"Yes, and we are very eager to have a child. We understood that it might be possible for a lesbian couple to adopt a child. Is there some problem with our relationship?"

This is not going well.

"Well, I. . .ummm. . .well. . .we. . .well. . .I've never met one before."

Gracie, this honest stuff isn't working. Help!!

As the conversation continued, we watched a possibly otherwise-competent social worker turn into a bumbling, horror-struck personality.

"Can you tell us what the best way would be for us to go about this? We are open to all children, but we are especially interested in a child from a foreign country. We have a friend who adopted a little girl, and she is so wonderful. Or is there another country that will allow a single-parent adoption?"

"Yes, some of the Central and South American countries allow single-parent adoptions, but. . .not two single women together. Let me go ask the director."

We waited for what seemed an interminable amount of time, oohing and aahing over the children's pictures placed by this agency and hung proudly about the room. We said nothing to each other, but the longer the caseworker was gone, the less each of us could imagine this agency placing a child like one of those in our home. . .with two mothers.

When the caseworker finally returned, she was so kind I could barely stomach it. The director had assured her they would have more information for us after they had some time to "research our case."

As we left the office, I glanced at a wall hanging: "The two most valuable gifts you can give a child are roots and wings."

We left there wondering if we could find a place to help give wings to our dream. Could we find an agency that would look past the fact that we were lesbians? Surely our desire and our abilities to parent would speak to someone somewhere.

We drove home from our first appointment feeling as if our wings had been clipped. Those doors flung open wide earlier in the day seemed to be closing on us.

Several weeks later we heard from the agency. They had decided that if we could find the baby, they would let us adopt it and do the proper paperwork for us. And take our money. From the telephone conversation it was clear we were to be treated as though litigation, not a child, was what we wanted. The attorney had been alerted — 'there are two crazy women loose in the area. They actually want to raise a child together. What is the world coming to? Next thing you know, they'll actually get one! Not with our names attached! This is a Christian organization. We only discriminate in the name of Jesus!'

"What we need them for is to find a baby. That's the whole point of going to an adoption agency."

"Yes, of course. In other words, they don't think two mothers are a good idea. . .especially the kind 'I've never met before,' but they won't come out and tell us no because they don't want a lawsuit. I want a baby, not a day in court! Now what?"

Perhaps we were naive to think others would be eager to help us in our dream. We assumed that with so many waiting children, there would be more willingness and less discrimination. We learned a great deal about adoption and truth and how to build a family during those months. The system is created to prevent adoption from taking place. I don't mean to be totally cynical, but the river to a successful adoption is strewn with one set of rapids after the other. It's hard for everyone unless one has lots of money. Even if one does come up with an entire life savings for the endeavor, one will need years of patience. People who fit the standard descriptions for adoptive parents — the right age, house, cash flow, religion, and sexual orientation — will still need large quantities of time, money, and patience. Others will find themselves becoming river guides, with tons of experience in steering a course through treacherous waters.

Somewhere in my heart I think that who Terryl and I are comes through to people. They can see that we have capitalized on our opportunities. We're educated, articulate, well-mannered, and clear-thinking enough to find our way to the right doors. We got the clear message, though, that we could be who we were if we didn't say so. If we let our opportunities show, if we played by the rules but hid our love — the very thing which most made us likely candidates to be good parents — then we could make it through the rugged course.

The truth is, I grew up in a heterosexual family; all of my lesbian friends did too — which is not to say that it always happens that way, but it is to say that people aren't lesbian because they are raised that way. I am lesbian because I was made that way; ask Gracie!

I suppose that people fear lesbian parents simply because they have never given a thought to how lesbians live and so it remains a mystery to them. Actually my life, our life together, is pretty much like everyone else's, even the woman's at the agency. We go to work, try to do well in our careers, struggle to find time for hobbies, enjoy getting together with friends, nurture our spiritual lives as best we can.

What makes a good parent isn't who we love but that we love. . .our children. . .with strong, faithful hearts and willingness to share life and opportunities with them and to learn from them.

But adoption and the system are not built on reason. When one is a lesbian, for many people the badge one wears overtakes the life one lives. We become just the label in some people's minds. The challenge is to wear the badge proudly and yet only give it the billing it deserves. The essential label for me is "mother."

We learned how to prioritize our needs and hold in our truth for the sake of a greater good. We determined shortly after this first disastrous interview that we would have to approach the adoption process as single women. We would have to hide our love and closeness for the sake of our child. Somehow we knew in this decision that we would have to choose this again and again. That experience brought other pain up for me.

Gracie, how can you love these people? And you need to know that it's asking just too much for me to love them. Touting all this holier-than-thou attitude, they leave people like us broken in pieces. Gracie, they all think they know how you live and who can come live with you. They figure you would never want me for a roommate. I stay as close as I can, and I know you're close to me, but they point and stare just like that woman at that agency. I feel like I might just as well take my clothes off. I feel abused and violated when people like that say they'll pray for me, when what they mean is that they'll pray I'll change my evil ways and become more like them. Oh, I know you want me to make room in my heart for them, but that attitude gripes me to the limit. Are you going to help us find a baby, or do we have to stand here naked forever?

I'm sorry, Gracie. I don't want to be angry. But I am. If I take my anger to them, I further distance myself.

Many in my family fade away when I try to tell them the truth. They don't ask me about my life with Terryl. I feel like an alien around them. They, like the rest of the world, act as if who I am and how I love Terryl is something to be avoided at all cost. They're nice enough, but not real enough. If only I could share the essence of our love and not have it misunderstood. I love like they do. I feel like they do. Why stare at the difference when the similarities are so many? I feel like the one common connection we have is you, but they don't know you the way I do. Isn't that the same thing they say about me? Help us blend. If I can love them, maybe they can love me. My family is so important to me. I don't want a baby for them. I want a baby for me. For us. But I want to raise our kids alongside theirs.

I want to raise my child in a world where our child won't bear the mark of two beasts. . . two mothers. It's very difficult to realize that we will be raising a child whom many will view as alien. It scares me to think that a small young life whom we will love could ever have to deal with such ignorance.

That's why it feels especially important to me that our families love our children. I want my child to be loved, not in spite of who we are but because a child, even one with us as parents, is meant to be loved and cherished, as we all are.

Oh, Gracie, are we asking too much this time? Can you move into this experience and touch the hearts of all of us? Please take my angry determination and give it a smile. Help me remember the humor in all of this. We'll take a child no one wants and love it. We'll give it a home and be loving parents. I will remember the humor. I will remember you. Got anything in your pocket for me?

Rest. . . love your family. They are only doing with you what they believe in their hearts. They, like you, are doing the very best they can. The woman at the agency is only doing her job. We have a lot of work to do in this world. Loving doesn't always feel good; it does take labor to love. I can only go where you are willing to take me. Take me into this journey, and together we will change as much as we can. You might want to thank them and love them all a whole lot more. Love is really all there is.

I know it sounds arrogant, but sometimes I think I take you places you've never been before. I mean I know we aren't the first couple of women who have looked for a child, and I know we are only just beginning, but this is the first time I've been here, and I want you to walk this virgin land with me. Hmmm...virgin land. Remember us now, virgin Mother. Was she really a virgin?

It wouldn't change the story one way or the other. Birth still happened. Jesus had a mother just like you, and she wasn't always delighted with what he had to do, but he did what he believed in. Think about that.

Yeah, but he was a man, and he could get away with it. Why didn't you send a girl baby?

Sugar, someday you'll learn it doesn't matter. It doesn't matter how you are, and it doesn't matter how Jesus came. People use Jesus because their own lives are so unlived and unhappy. They look to him for their salvation when I'm inside beating on their hearts trying to get through. People argue about differences and make them into a big deal so they will have another excuse for being separate.

You get separated from your parents, your sister, and your brother because you're a lesbian, and they see you through a lens conditioned by years of misunderstanding. And your niece and nephews think you're odd and try to figure out ways to talk about you to their children. You stand around in my house and debate the silliest things because you all see religion as some kind of eternal answer. It's a placebo for love. Then you come to me complaining because you, like them, think someone else is wrong about something. It goes on and on endlessly.

And then, as if that weren't enough, women wish Jesus was a woman so they could get more understanding, and men like it the way it is because it gives them an edge. And then they take advantage of a dishonest system they've created to keep the separation ongoing. The distance continues, and the separation grows. And all the time I just want you to love each

27

other. It really is a hard thing to do. You're all one. All the stuff you think makes you so different from each other is what is most common in each of you. You each want to be loved and loveable. If you could get that. . . the rest of it really doesn't matter.

I hope you'll use this gift from my pocket. . . it's one of the best I have to give.

Thanks, Gracie. Can I have a hug? Someday I'm going to hug you in person.

That's for sure! Until then, go hug T.

My pleasure.

Mine too!

* * *

We decided to put off the notion of adoption for the moment and began looking into the possibility of donor insemination. We had seesawed between adoption and donor insemination all along. We both wanted to experience giving birth, and yet we always felt that there were already so many children who needed homes. We wanted so to share our lives with them. But when adoption seemed blocked, we decided to take the path of least resistance first.

We found a fertility clinic with a sperm bank nearby and did some reading on the procedure for woman-assisted insemination. We purchased all the necessary equipment and began testing for the exact time of ovulation. We began to connect with all the women in the world who have tried and who are trying to bring a child into the world. The real miracle of life is the stubborn insistence of the few to bring about the many.

We talked about donor insemination for hours and hours. We learned to balk at the term "artificial insemination" because there is nothing artificial about the process or the elements used. We are real persons, the sample is real sperm, the people who dream are real people.

We mastered ovulation predictor kits. We stood on our heads — figuratively as well as literally — injecting sample after sample. We kept the faith through the difficult moment each month when the pregnancy test stayed clear instead of turning blue, which it is supposed to do if the test is positive.

It was such an exciting time. Every month we felt this incredible rush of life, imagining that Terryl might be pregnant.

We decided to go through a clinic where the donor remains anonymous to us rather than connecting with a male friend because we did not want to deal with issues of paternity. We wanted to be the parents. We didn't want to share that. Of course, we talked for hours about how important it might be for our child to know a father, but we concluded that many children grow up without fathers present in their homes or in their lives and they do just fine. We wanted our child to have good solid male influence and relationships, but we figured that could come through other channels.

We asked the hard questions: Should we not have children because we don't have a man in our lives? Should we not consider parenthood because the child will be harmed or slighted? We decided that we were living proof that happiness, love, sharing, family, and life in abundance are available outside the norm. We decided that what we have to offer — in terms of love, caring, sharing, and family nurture — far exceeds any liabilities that could possibly arise through donor insemination.

We searched out a clinic noted for both their rigorous screening of donors and their careful testing of the sperm samples. We asked them the tough questions: Will you be able to deal with us as a couple? Will you allow both of us to be present for the procedure? Will you treat us with the same kindness and respect as any other couple? Will you be just as eager to work with us to achieve pregnancy as you would with any other couple?

* * *

On a rare Sunday home for me, we were lounging around, reading the paper. Suddenly I had this overwhelming sense that a child was near to us somehow. We had just "tested clear" a few days earlier, but I felt an unmistakeable sense of pending delivery.

"Honey, what do you say we take a couple weeks' vacation? I have this very strong feeling that we don't have much time left to go on that European vacation we've always wanted. I get the strange feeling that it's now or never. . .like we're going to be blessed with a baby sometime soon."

"Well, maybe it would be a good idea. Too bad that theory about getting pregnant on vacation when the stress is less won't work for us! Let's go."

* * *

29

Four days after returning from Europe, I was sitting in my office when the phone rang.

It was Barb and Rachel. Their friend's daughter, Susan, was pregnant. Susan, a senior in high school, told her mother she didn't feel ready to keep a child. She was just two months along.

Earlier that same month, Barb and Rachel had come to California to visit us. Susan and her mother flew in from San Francisco to spend a day with them. One night during that visit we had a festive celebration of Rachel's pregnancy! After her earlier ectopic pregnancy, she had finally become properly pregnant, again by insemination. We were all so relieved and happy for them.

After the call from Barb and Rachel, I went back in my memory to that party. I remembered Susan's silence. No wonder. . .she was also pregnant at the time but hiding her secret.

"It's a good thing we went to Europe, T! That's a tough trip to take with an infant!"

"This is so exciting. What do you think? Should we follow up on this?"

The question was rhetorical. We both knew we were well into a seven-month labor.

We stopped inseminating, not feeling prepared to deal with two infants at once. Not long after the first call we met with Susan and her mother. We began making decisions and preparing for the pending blessed event. We spoke with Susan and her family often on the phone. We drove up to San Fransisco to take Susan out for a special dinner on her birthday about a month before her due date. We felt very good all along about our connection with her, and we were growing more and more anxious for our little child with every passing day.

Waiting was so difficult. One of our happiest times was a baby shower our friends gave for us. They went out of their way to make sure that this baby would be equipped with the best of everything! The cake was decorated with a shooting star and the message, "Dreams do come true!" We both agreed we had never been to a party we more enjoyed!

The flood continued forty days upon the earth; and the waters increased, and bore up the ark, and it rose high above the earth (Gen. 7:17).

We were in the river. . .

30

afterbirth

At the end of forty days Noah opened the window of the ark which he had made...(Gen. 8:6).

We left our faceprints on the nursery window the early morning of our son's birth, trying to get as close to him as they would allow us. There had been some hitch in the system somewhere. Apparently, the fact that this was an adoption had not been communicated through the proper channels, and the nursing staff would not allow us to get near him.

"This is insane. It's a little hard to get papers from our attorney at two o'clock in the morning. Can't you trust our word? Bonding is so very important at a time like this for both the child and us. Here is the Grandmother of this child asking you to let us begin bonding with the child, and you refuse to listen."

"Which one of you is the adopting parent?"

"We both are."

We shouldn't have said that.

It was only after our insistence that Mrs. Munez was allowed to hold him. She tried to sneak him out to us on the other side of the window, but the sergeant-at-arms caught her.

"No one is to hold this child except you. Until we have a written relinquishment or verbal approval from the birth mother, no one is allowed to hold this child. We will no longer allow you to hold him if you attempt to take him from this room."

We left the hospital shortly before sunrise of our little boy's birthday. There was no point in trying to make sense of a crazy system, and we figured we would need some rest to face it again later in the morning.

"Relax now, Honey. Mrs. Munez said she would talk with Susan as soon as she wakes up and get her to sign the release papers."

"Do you believe her?"

"Might as well believe her. I just feel horrible that our son has to lie there crying with no one to hold him. That's worth a few months of therapy down the road."

"Maybe we can help to quell that feeling of abandonment within him. Chances are he's a more-than-average survivor to have chosen us for parents. I mean, let's face it, two mothers. I understand they give you tickets for that in some places."

"Silly, let's get some rest now. Today is going to be a big day."

"I can't sleep! I just keep seeing that little buddy wailing through the window."

"I can't sleep either. I'm scared."

"What are you scared about, Honey?"

"Well, I've never been a mother before. I've never had a little boy before. You know, I thought he was going to be a girl. I remember all the stories my mother has told me about how she thought I was going to be a boy. Either Joel or David. When they told her she had twins, she was delighted. One will be Joel, and one will be David. Oops. . .twin girls. No wonder it took her a couple weeks to name us. Naming has been a trip, huh, Honey? I mean we have done names from Denver to Paris to California and back and forth with every person with whom we've come into contact for the past five years. Do you think everybody has such a tough time naming their kid? Do you know now what you want to name him? I just want to give him a name he'll love. I'd just hate it if, after all this, we would name him something the kids at school would give him a hard time about. Of course they teased me, and Judy is totally common and ordinary. Will they give our son a hard time about his name? On top of having two mothers and his first several hours unattended, does he stand a chance? Will he be abnormal? Will he want to be a police officer? Or will we find him dead on some

32

cold, lonely freeway someday? Oh, God, T. Are we doing the right thing, I mean, can we do this? I mean, I think I'm losing my mind."

"I think you are, too. Now would you just rest and go to sleep? Honey, we've been around and around all these issues for years. Yes, all of the above is possible. Let's wait until we hold him. We'll name him then, and we'll all feel much better."

* * *

"What time is it?"

"Oh, my God, it's 9:30. Gotta get up."

"Well, we didn't go to sleep until six, so we haven't exactly been irresponsible. Let's get a move on. We're supposed to be at the hospital in an hour."

When we arrived, we were met by the day nurse. She greeted us warmly and led us immediately to the infant care room. She took us right to our son's crib and left us alone with him.

We lifted him from the crib together, and both of us left tears on his tightly wrapped blanket. We kissed his little face and loosened the blanket from around him.

"This is what they must mean by 'swaddling.'"

"What's your name, little baby boy?"

"I think he's Noah."

"What does that name mean again?"

"Noah means 'wandering' and 'rest.'"

"After your nine months of wandering, come and rest in our lives. Yeah, Noah! I think he likes his name."

"Welcome to our lives, dearest little Noah."

"And look at these teensy little fingernails! Maybe he's going to be a pianist or a doctor."

"How about if he just gets to be our baby for awhile. I promise you can take him to his first interview at three. Until then, he's homebound, grounded without parole."

"Look at his toes, Honey! And these little knees. He could never be a police officer with knees like this."

"It's a good thing. We've already had this discussion. I wish we could take him off somewhere by ourselves and talk to him. See if he likes his name. Does he look like a Noah? I mean, do you think he can swim?"

33

"With knees like that? Great for swimming. Just not so hot for running after criminals."

"He'll need them for praying though if he's going to make it through a system like this. Could you believe all the hurdles? Noah, did you know how much we wanted to hold you during those first few hours of your life when they let you just lie in the bassinet and cry? It broke our hearts to watch you through the window, but they wouldn't let us in. They weren't told we were your new mothers."

"What a wonderful sound! I can hardly wait to get him home with us. He feels so good to hold. All my fears have just faded away. It's like the three of us together can do anything. Oh, little boy, Noah, do you know how much we have wanted you? Do you know how long we have looked for you?"

"Here's his formula. Be sure you stop after he's had one third of the bottle and burp him because he has such a little tummy. Then feed him as much of the rest of the bottle as he will take. You can come back for his feedings each morning and once at night until he is released from the hospital. With adoptions, unless previous arrangements have been made, the baby cannot be released until the birth mother is released. Since his birth mother had a C-section, you can probably count on being here with him for another four or five days. The social worker is on the first floor around by the business office. She called to say she can meet with you at noon. He's a real beauty. Is this the first child for you?"

"Yes, thank you."

"I'm sure glad the other nurse went home. This nurse is the first decent person we've run into in this hospital. He's hungry, isn't he? What a beautiful, adorable, wonderful child! Our son. What do you think, Bunkie?"

"I think I'm the happiest person in the world."

"Me too! Can I come along and share the happiest spot in the world with you?"

"As long as you bring Noah."

Gracie, this is the moment. Thank you, thank you for hearing us and for keeping us close for the moment. I'm certainly glad you're more powerful than the system.

"We have to go now, Honey. Little Noah, we'll be back in a few hours. We love you. Always remember, you didn't grow under our hearts but in them."

"The birth mother is having a very difficult time. She has called her boyfriend, and he is scheduled to be here tomorrow morning to meet his son."

"What? She hasn't seen him since she got pregnant. We thought everything was resolved. We spent so much time with her before this delivery. We always saw her as a child, and we loved her. We talked about her boyfriend and her loss and her loneliness. This is very confusing."

"Well, as long as she is in this hospital, she calls the shots and the child is under her custody. She told me she has worked with you over the past six months and had decided to adopt her child out to you, but she isn't sure now. She has decided you can see the baby two feeding times each day. I have spoken with your attorney, and she is preparing to call Susan to get some word from her. You can reach her later today. Your attorney told me she has met with both Susan alone and with Susan and her mother in addition to the time when the three of you set up the original adoption conference. The bottom line is, though, no matter what preliminary work your attorney did, the ball is in Susan's court. I've seen a lot of these independent adoptions, and they can be very tricky. My advice to you is that you come in for the feedings, and otherwise keep a low profile. These adoptions can be very messy, and until she hands the baby to you out in front of the hospital upon her release, I wouldn't count on this for sure. Now I have another appointment. Good day."

We spent the time before connecting with our attorney arranging to have a kite made for Noah across the Bay in Sausalito. We walked aimlessly in and out of the village's shops, trying to keep our minds active and encouraging ourselves to be positive and hopeful.

The call from the attorney came a hundred years later in the day.

"But is there nothing else we can do? I mean, this little boy already means everything to us. He's been ours in our minds for years. And now to hold him and maybe lose him so soon. It can't be happening."

"Hold on. All you can do is wait and hope that Susan keeps her original promise. Ride it out. Keep busy with something else. Go shopping or to the movies or out to dinner. If she decides to relinquish him, you only have a couple of nights left to be alone together and to get some sleep. Believe me, I know. Once you have a baby, you'll cherish the memory of your last few quiet nights together."

We cared a great deal for Susan, but it was hard to feel so much for someone else when our hearts were resting on her decision. We had read a lot about young mothers who give up their children, and we knew the loss she would feel should she ultimately decide to relinquish Noah to us. There was considerable conflict in this moment, knowing that it is dangerous territory to ask someone to do something you would have so much trouble doing yourself. Our every thought for the next four days was consumed with Susan and Noah.

* * *

We stood outside the hospital the day Susan was released with our hearts showing in our throats. The last we had heard she was planning to continue with the adoption. That was last night. This morning everything could have changed. The meeting with the boyfriend was apparently not everything she had hoped. She was sore and tired and wanted to get back to school as soon as possible. High school graduation was just seven months away, and she wanted to get back with her class. Our conversations were by phone each time, but judging from her voice, she sounded certain about her decision.

"Here he comes."

Oh Gracie, please let this happen.

He was dressed in an outfit from the shower and wrapped in the baby blanket I had knitted for him.

Very quickly, Susan handed Noah to us and tearfully said, "Please take good care of him."

"We will. You have made us the happiest people in the world. We will not disappoint you. He is so beautiful, and we love him so much already. We love you, too, Susan."

Grandmother and Great-Grandmother stood beside Susan. We all hugged one another. Great-Grandmother came over to us and said, "Ever since the first day I met you, I knew this baby would be very lucky. Tell him about me."

Susan's mother came over to us then and said, "This is best. I'm glad for you."

36

We all cried.

Only Noah was left, and those that were with him in the ark (Gen. 7:23).

The midwives gathered him up from the river.

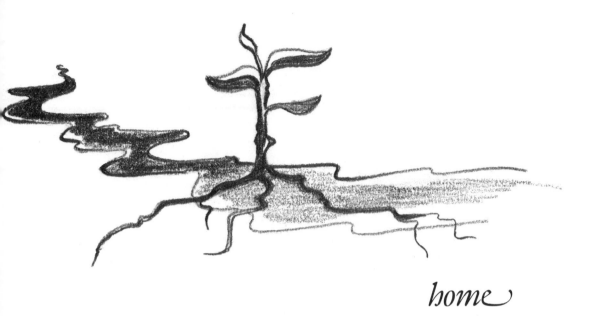

home

We left the hospital with so many mixed feelings. We were exhausted from the emotional ordeal of the past five days, concerned about Susan and her feelings, and mostly delighted to have our son with us and to be on our way home.

Arriving at the airport gave us our first lesson in juggling baby equipment and luggage. We silently realized that our trips would be numbered from now on.

Terryl's sister, who lives in the Bay Area, had come to meet us and to be introduced to her new nephew. It was a moment to cherish.

As we were sitting in the airport restaurant, a tour of Japanese salesmen made a parade around our table, no doubt wondering where the papa was.

We were lugging our "household" to the departure gate when I spotted Susan and Mrs. Munez coming in our direction.

"Oh, no, Terryl, look . . ."

"Well, what are you doing here? Is everything okay?"

Mrs. Munez could see the terror in our eyes.

"Oh, no, no, everything is fine. We just came to pick up a friend of mine. I had no idea you were leaving from this terminal. I should have said something to you earlier. Everything is fine."

They greeted Noah awkwardly, and Mrs. Munez whisked Susan away to the next gate. We gathered our piles of equipment and hurried into the jetway as soon as our flight was called.

"That was strange."

"Yeah, let's get home safe where we belong."

* * *

He looked like a little angel resting on Terryl's shoulder as the plane took off. We were both beyond emotional exhaustion, but our hearts were whole and our dreams were soaring.

"No holding back now, Bunkie! We've got our little boy, and we're on our way. Would you look at this face! What an angel! He really is a beauty. Thank God for that one kind nurse."

Thanks, Gracie. Oh, my God, thank you for this moment. Thank you for the dream of my lifetime. How can I say thanks? Thank you, thank you, thank you, forever, and ever, and ever.

"Would you like something to drink? Your little baby is beautiful. How old is he?"

Here comes the first look of the unbelieving. "He's just five days old."

"Five days, wow! You sure are looking good for just five days after birth. After I had my first child, I looked like a tank for a month."

"Well, he's adopted."

"Isn't that nice! Would you like something to drink?"

"Yes, I always get so thirsty in flight. Could I have a can of diet soda?"

"Sure. Good luck with the baby."

"Can you believe we actually have him in our arms, and we're on our way home? Yeah, we made it, Bunkie! He must be hungry. He always cries when he's hungry. Remember yesterday morning when we fed him, and he cried so hard before the nurse gave us the bottle?"

"There, that's all it takes."

I have never seen clouds like this before. They are so beautiful and fluffy. That one looks like a reindeer. Christmas is going to be amazing this year. Look at this wonderful child. I bet he looks just like Jesus did. Maybe he is Jesus. He feels so marvelously special to me. I have a feeling that his being Noah is every bit as special as it was for Jesus to be Jesus. I think that's what Jesus tried to say. Right, Gracie? There's a Santa cloud. Better catch up with those reindeer! We'll do the nursery first, then put up the tree.

Judy, this is only October!

But today feels so much like Christmas. Isn't that the day we get everything we want? Just look at this little guy! And there's Terryl looking like she's been a mommy forever. I feel like I'm going to bust. The nursery. No, we'll do that after our visitors come so they have a place to sleep. The crib is on layaway until later in November, so we can keep him in our room in the bassinet. We have enough stuffed animals and cute little baby things to make this nursery a great little home for our Noah. Our Noah, is that a new song? He is so adorable. So is Terryl. What a family!

"Ouch! And just what are you doing?"

"I just wanted to pinch you to see if you were real. Can you believe this?"

All right, Gracie. Good work.

"I can't wait for the first time he calls me 'Mommy.' Being someone's Mom is a big deal. Here we are. You'd think I was the first mother to have ever lived. Today I feel so special and alive and excited. Don't you, Honey?"

"Yes. And I feel very tired. Let's get our stuff and get off this bird."

* * *

The Coast Highway didn't look quite this lovely on the trip up. I'm not sure I even saw it, I was going so fast. It looks more beautiful than ever before. Look at that ocean! All rivers lead to this point. We put our dream into the river, and we got the ocean. A baby boy. This is all so thrilling. I wonder what my mother will think? Love him, Mother. Love him and be a proud Grandma. I'll make you proud of me. I'll be a great parent, and Terryl and I will be great with our kid. Don't worry. He'll be terrific, well-adjusted, well-loved, and the world will soften about us. . .one by one. . .you'll see. Gracie. . .

"What are you thinking about?"

"I was wondering how Mom and Dad will do with little Noah. I want them to really think he's terrific. I want them to think we're terrific, too."

"We'll find out soon enough."

"Jan will be here the day after tomorrow. I like it that my twin wants to come help out right away."

"He's sound asleep back there. He has the most beautiful complexion. Japanese and Portugese is a great combination. It looks very good on our little Noah. I hope Dad won't get freaked with his ethnicity. I'll just tell Dad he's Gracie's son. Gracie, the Mother of us all!"

"Yeah, and then you'll have all that to explain! Don't worry. Your father will be wild about him."

"We're home, little Noah. Come on, come meet your two little doggies."

"Trevor, Chelsea, come here. Oh, we missed you too. Here, Honey, can you put Noah up on the chair before Trevor licks his face off. Yes, good boy, we missed you too. Chelsea, come here. Are you still pouting? We're home now. Look overjoyed. I want you to meet our new 'little puppy.'"

"I don't think Chelsea's very interested. Give her a treat, and she'll be happy. Come on, little Noah, let's show you your new home. This is your ocean. See, you can look out this window and see the whales going down the coast in the spring, and we'll show you the pelicans and the seagulls and the seals. And here is our living room where we want you to come and live with us. And this is our bedroom. We're going to share it with you for the next couple of weeks until your Aunt Jan and your new Grandma and Grandpa come to visit. And, see, this will be your room real soon. He's hungry again, Honey. Can you hand me his bottle?"

* * *

"I'll get the phone. Hello. Yes! He's here!"

"Isn't he wonderful? Jan, you're just going to love him! I can't wait for you to get here. Yes, I'll pick you up. Yes, I'll have Noah with me. He's not quite old enough to leave alone!"

* * *

"Jannie, welcome! Here's our little Noah."

"Oh, Judy. Oh my! Oh. . .Oh, he's so beautiful! Oh my!"

"People are always so articulate around little babies. Oh oh, goo goo, woo woo."

"Stop! He's just such a little doll! Is he good?"

"Good? He's great. He's the best little boy in America. In the world. Right, Mr. Noah? Come on, let's get your stuff and go play with our little guy."

Noah was a very alert and active baby. One day he would sleep a few hours at night, and the next he would stay awake endlessly. We took shifts at night so that one of us could try to sleep through the night while the other one responded to his needs. While Jan was with us, she took turns too. I never felt closer to my twin sister. I felt like she was loving Noah just like I did. It was fun to watch her. Sort of like watching a home movie. Is that me or Jan? It's still a little spooky to have someone around who looks so much like me! It was great to watch her fall in love with Noah. I saw some of myself in those charming days. The memories are written on my heart.

I remember the morning we tried all of his clothes on him in one sitting. Poor little boy! Everything was so cute, and he looked so adorable in each little outfit. He put up with us while we picked our favorites.

His first bath was an exercise in howling for him and weeping for us. We didn't like it that he didn't like it, but we had to try out that new little plastic tub. This was one ark Noah wanted no part of. It really would have made a better bird bath. He just howled.

Rock him gently, faithful Gracie. Sing him soft, a lullaby. Shower him with tender mercy; keep the soap out of his eyes. Treat him kindly in this water; heal his young, deserving soul. Build a world where peace shall greet him; mold his heart out of your smile. Let this water be the river where we offer him to you. Keep him safe with us forever, a family now and ever more. Rock him gently, faithful Gracie; give your mother's heart to me. Teach me how to love him gently, as you rock us in your arms. Let us rest inside a pocket in your skirt so soft and warm. Thank you, Gracie, for this moment. You have blessed us. "Precious Son, cry no more."

We filled a photograph album the first week. "Here's Noah getting up. Here he is hungry. Here he is waking up. And smiling — it must be gas. And wailing. . .eating. . .burping. . .resting. . .looking at us like, 'if you take one more picture of me, I'm going to throw up on the lens.' "

It didn't take long for us to become dragons.

"How you doing, Honey?"

"I'm just dragging."

I had a week-long meeting and a weekend meeting out of town just a couple of weeks after we brought him home.

"How's our little buddy? I miss you both so much. This is double the grief I usually feel. Now I have two of you away from me."

Once the meetings were over, I had carved out a couple of weeks in my calendar to be with Noah and Terryl. Mom and Dad were scheduled to arrive two days after I returned — one day to get the house in shape and one day to oogle over my baby. The oogling was great.

* * *

"Oh, he's just beautiful! And you have him in that little outfit I sent. He's big, huh, Honey? What was he, almost ten pounds? See, you and Jannie were only about five each, so he's as big as you both were together! The house just looks beautiful. There's the phone, I'll get it."

"No, this is her mother. Well, we just got here and . . . okay, if it's important. Judy, there's a woman on the phone, and she says it's very important she talk with you right away. I'm sorry. I tried to discourage her, but she said she had to talk to you."

"That's okay, Mom. It's probably just one of my pastors who is having some trouble in their church."

"Hello, this is Judy. Oh, well, how are you, Mrs. Munez? What's up?"

He waited another seven days, and again he sent forth the dove out of the ark; and the dove came back to him in the evening, and lo, in her mouth, a freshly plucked olive leaf; so Noah knew that the waters had subsided from the earth. Then he waited another seven days, and sent forth the dove; and she did not return to him any more (Gen. 8:10-12).

Must we build a basket and waterproof it from the river?

the flood

"Judy, what's wrong? Judy, talk to me! Elmer, something terrible has just happened! Judy is in the bathroom crying her heart out. Here, hold Noah."

"Sure. What's the matter?"

"I don't know. I'm going to go find out. He is such a beautiful baby! Look at him! Okay, just hold him. He'll be good."

"Honey, what's wrong? Oh, Honey, tell me. Should I call Terryl? Is she okay?

"Oh, it's okay. You don't have to tell me yet. There, there. Is Terryl okay? Thank God. Okay, take a breath. Breathe, Judy, you're forgetting to breathe. That won't help. There, that's good. Well, Honey, you're just sweating. Shhh . . ."

"That . . . that was Mrs. Munez . . ."

"Uh huh, go ahead. Oh, Honey, breathe."

"She wants our . . . our . . ."

"Oh, no, they want Noah? Elmer, they want Noah back! Oh Darling, oh Judy, maybe they'll change their minds."

"Do you think they might?"

"Sure. Yes, this can't happen. Come on, let's go sit on the sofa. Can I get you something? Elm, go get Judy a glass of water. How's our little Noah?"

"Okay, he's fine. Judy, he's a good little baby, isn't he? Judy, I'm so sorry. Here's some water. Can I get you something else? Do you want to hold Noah?"

"Only if I can keep him forever. Oh, Mother, this can't be happening. She said she's trying to talk Susan out of this. Mrs. Munez is upset, too. She's wanted us to have the baby all along. She's been terrific through the whole thing — the Great-Grandmother, too. But she says that Susan is determined and that neither she nor anyone else is going to change Susan's mind. She wanted to call me before Susan does, to warn us. Oh my God, Mom, what am I going to tell Terryl?"

"Elm, go get some tissues, would you? Oh Honey, you're going to call Terryl and tell her what just happened. Then we'll all work this out together. Do you want me to call her?"

"No, that's okay, Mom. I better call her."

"May I please speak with Terryl? Thank you."

"Honey, hi. This is Judy. Ummm, I just got a phone call from Mrs. Munez, and oh...and a...Susan wants Noah back. I know. Okay. Please do."

"She's on her way home. She says it's going to be okay. I feel better now. Where's my boy? Hi, little darling."

"Noah, Noah, little Noah, we love you. You're the very best by far. Yes, you are. You're our baby, and we love you now and forever more. Little Noah, you're a blessing. Yes, you are. We love you too, oh, yes, we do...when no-o-thing else would do, yooooou came hooome too."

"That's the little song we sing to him first thing every morning."

"That's such a sweet song, Judy."

"Oh, Noah, we won't let you go; we just won't. Okay, now let's wipe up these tears and get on with this welcoming party. Here, Mom and Dad, let's get your suitcase upstairs. You can unpack while I tend to Noah's drawers. I think he's just reacted to the news in a big way, if you know what I mean. Come on, little guy."

Gracie, tell me this isn't happening. I am not believing this. I just got all of my meetings out of the way and was settling into some precious time with my son, and now this phone call! I'm going to act like it's a nightmare. It _is_ a nightmare. You can't mean this. You don't mean this.

Sugar, I have nothing to do with this. I'm not a monster, lurking in the corner, waiting to pounce on you and give you a hard time. I love you.

I ached right along with you during that phone call. It made me feel sick inside. I just finished wiping my tears on my skirt next to yours. I'm with you. Right now, so is your little Noah. Let's keep believing. Don't believe I'm the cause of this. I always believe in you. I rock you gently, just like you ask, all of you together. Easy, Sugar.

"Noah, I hear your other mommy coming. Yup, here she is. Hi, Honey. Are we going to be okay? Thanks for coming home."

"Of course. Hi, little guy. He looks so cute. Hi, Jayne. Hi, Elmer. What a welcome, huh? Yes, I really do think everything is going to be okay. Susan is just going through what all mothers who give up children must go through. She'll get to the other side of this immediate grief and realize what she did originally. It is very difficult for a seventeen-year-old to take care of a baby. Especially when her mother will not allow her to live at home with him. Mrs. Munez has raised her children. Now she is going to remarry. She wants to have her own life with her new husband. It will all work out. But it is a terrible scare. We just have to keep our thoughts positive and our prayers strong. What do you say we make the most of this day with Noah. She may never even call."

We spent the afternoon and well into the evening talking with Mom and Dad. They were absolutely wonderful with us and with Noah. We talked about our ambivalence about adoption early on precisely because of the risks involved in independent adoptions. We tried to remember the difficult time Susan was going through, but it had come as such a shock. We had really felt that we were safe once we brought Noah home.

* * *

"Hello. Hi, Susan. Yes, your mother called earlier."

"Are you sure? But Susan, have you really thought this through?"

"Well, I know he's coming back around, and he thinks he wants to raise his son, but you never heard from him for six months while you were pregnant."

"It sounds like he just wants to play house. Where will you live?"

"Does he have a job? Well, then how are you going to care for your son?"

"But welfare is a pretty tough road, and you can't work a full-time job if you're going to school."

47

"Oh, Susan, you don't want to drop out this close to graduation. You're only a few months away."

"Look, we talked with you for months leading up to this. You promised us you would not come back for Noah. . . . Well, that's the name we've given him. You said you wouldn't come back for the baby once you placed him in our arms. Please, don't do this. Please think this through."

"How can you be so sure now, Susan? You said you were sure when you gave him to us just a month ago at the hospital."

"But we've built our lives around this little boy."

"Yes, I know, but you told us you wanted more for him than you felt you could give. What has changed since then?"

"Oh, Susan, Jeff will come around until you bring the baby home, and after the first week of no sleep and no money and no more going out when he wants because he has to babysit while you're working, he'll split."

"Well, I think you're fooling yourself."

"Look, Susan, we don't believe this would be in the best interest of the baby. We're going to talk to our attorney and see what we can do to keep him."

"Well, we're not going to just hand him over because you've changed your mind again. He's not a ping-pong ball."

"From now on, you can speak to our attorney."

* * *

"I feel so awful, talking to her that way, but what else can we do? I know, but we've loved her through all this too, and she has blessed us with this priceless treasure. Oh, I don't know, Mother. We'll have to see what Ruth thinks. Yes, she's our attorney. I can't think any more. This is so draining. Little Noah, can we sleep tonight?"

* * *

"Ruth got a letter today from a social worker in their county. It is official. They want him back. She says California has absolutely no protection for adopting parents in situations where the birth mother changes her mind. She says the longer we can hold onto him, the better the chance that Susan will change her mind again. So I say, let's hold on."

"This scares me so much. I feel so very sad. We've just got to figure something out."

48

"We will. Why don't you call your Mom? She'll want to know. They were so great during their visit."

"We had waited with such joy for them to meet their new grandson. Maybe Gracie will find another pocket in her skirt with a big miracle."

This is agony, Gracie. I have so many mixed feelings. One minute I'm just sure Susan will change her mind; the next minute I hope I wake up from this terrible nightmare. I'm afraid to believe it. I'm afraid not to believe it. Every day, he's more a part of us. I thought I'd bust right out of my clothes last night in the grocery store when that woman said he looked like me. If we become even more of each other, it will just keep getting harder every day to let go. Oh, do I have to let go? Of Noah? Not Noah! I let go of T, and she came back. But will the river be so kind this time? What about T? She is absolutely in love with him. It's bad enough dealing with this myself, but looking at T and watching her hope slide into the river too is almost more than I can bear. Do we have to put him in the river? Will the Pharoah's daughter have compassion on him? If we fight to keep him, the judge will only see two lesbians. We won't look like mothers; we'll look like dragons. Oh, Gracie, how can we let go? I think my heart is breaking. I think a part of me is dying.

I remembered a part of the story from <u>A Raisin in the Sun</u>, and I went off to look it up after Ruth called that morning:

Child, when do you think is the time to love somebody the most; when they done good and made things easy for everybody? Well then, you ain't learning — because that ain't the time at all. It's when [s]he's at [her] lowest and can't believe in [her]self 'cause the world done whipped [her] so.[1]

* * *

Just two days after we heard that Susan wanted Noah back, we got a call from a Denver hospital. Rachel had just given birth to a little girl! Life is so full of mixed blessings. I wanted to rejoice so with Barb and Rachel. It was very difficult to do. As they were saying hello, we were saying goodbye.

[1] From Lorraine Hansberry, *A Raisin in the Sun* (New York: Random House, 1959), Act 3. Copyright © 1958 by Robert Nemiroff, as an unpublished work. Copyright © 1959, 1966, 1984 by Robert Nemiroff.

I felt so bonded to women who have lost a child and who had to let it go. I felt like Jochabed was my sister, Gracie our mother, and all the women through time from then until now were holding us and keeping us close for the journey. I felt such an ambivalence about Susan. How hard it had been for her to relinquish her child. Now we were sharing the same grief.

* * *

I put all of Noah's clothes and toys in a big bag. I kept a few things out just in case we ever dared to dream again. I would give the world for another precious, tragic day. I packed away the bassinet and anything that would remind us of him when we got home from this last journey with our son, knowing he would live forever in our hearts' home where memories never die. We put him in his favorite little outfit and sat on the sofa, the five of us together, looking at our ocean. Trevor was still licking him, Chelsea just wanted another bone. Together, we held him and shared our final secret blessing meant only for him. The one who brought him to us was calling out his name.

We would never build that castle in the sand. He wouldn't see the whales this spring. Christmas shouldn't have to come this year. Thanksgiving is the day after tomorrow.

* * *

Our attorney looked sick. The social worker tried to ease the moment.

"This happens a lot these days. More and more, even very young mothers want to keep their babies. I'm sure you gave him a wonderful start. I think it was wise for you to decide not to see Susan."

"Yes, they're here for him."

What happens to a dream deferred?
Does it dry up
Like a raisin in the sun?[2]

We all cried.

[2] Reprinted from THE PANTHER AND THE LASH, Langston Hughes, by permisson of Alfred A. Knopf, Inc., New York. Copyright © 1951 by Langston Hughes.

And rain fell upon the earth forty days and forty nights (Gen. 7:12).
Gracie. . .
Come on, Sugar, I'll walk you to the river.
And we placed him in a basket made from our dreams and gave him
to the river.

broken windows

November 22, 1985

Dear Friends and Family:

Just six and a half short weeks ago, we were sending you cards to announce the birth of our son, Noah. Since that time we have been family; we have loved him with our lives. Noah has touched us with his life in ways we will always cherish. We trust that we have given him the kind of love and care during this time which will provide a foundation for his growth.

About two weeks ago the birth mother called to say she wanted him back, that she had changed her mind. During this time we have tried, with our attorney, to turn things around so that we could keep Noah home with us. We were unable to do that. Today at ten-thirty we are returning Noah to his biological parents.

Our hearts are broken. We are so sad. We are writing this letter to all of you because it is such a tender thing for us to talk about. As time goes by and we feel stronger, we will feel better about talking. We also feel the sadness of so many of you who have waited with us for Noah, who have loved him through us, and those of you who have been blessed by meeting him. We are so sorry this is so sad for so many.

This morning as we awakened with our son, holding him in these last few hours, we were very in touch with your love and your support for us and all that you mean to each of us. Thank you for waiting and praying with us. Thank you for loving us through this difficult time. Thank you for giving us the kind of hope and love we both need so much right now.

Please join us in sending love and all of God's best blessings to our little Noah. Keep him in your prayers, please. Please remember his biological parents as well. May they be filled with the kind of gifts Noah needs in his young life.

Having <u>you</u> in our lives is so wonderful and gives us so much to be thankful for. Happy Thanksgiving to each of you. Even with this broken dream . . .you make it a beautiful world.

Our love,

Judy and Terryl

* * *

On that day all the fountains of the great deep burst forth, and the windows of the heavens were opened (Gen. 7:11).

It was a silent ride home along the coast. The ocean had a haze wrapped around it. The beauty of our ride just six and a half weeks earlier had faded into the river.

We looked at each other without words, reached for our jackets from the backseat of the car, gathered our broken dreams, and headed for the ocean path. The day crashed into our lives like the intense winter tide.

Walking arm-in-arm, Terryl and I dismissed the stares of passers-by. We walked the beach for hours, numb, beginning our distant love affair with a little boy who came into our lives bringing the end of the flood and the beginning of the rain. We began then to hold him where motherless children keep their silent connection, a place where even the rain will not wash him from our memory, knowing with each step left in the sand we would never be the same again.

Let me wash away your tears, my gentle mother-friends. Today I call you sisters, for we share the moment of giving a son to the river. I will sing your little Noah a lullaby for you this evening. . . Noah, Noah, little Noah, they love you. You're the very best by far. Yes, you are. They were

54

mommies, and I sing this song for them to you. They will always love you, Noah, you will love them too. They love you true. Oh yes, they do. . .When nothing else will help, they love you true.

Gracie, give him wings. Sing to him often of our love.

When we got home from our walk on the beach that afternoon, we found a large box that had been left for us in the courtyard — addressed to "Mr. Noah." Later that day another delivery came — the kite we had specially made for him the day he was born. He would never fly that kite, nor ride the swing that had come in the other box.

* * *

"Mom, he's gone."

"Jannie, please don't cry so hard. . . . I'm so sorry."

"Oh, Honey, I wish it didn't have to hurt them so much. Jan couldn't even talk. You call your family, and then let's unplug the phone for a year."

* * *

Somehow we made it through Thanksgiving and Christmas. I don't remember exactly how. Not until mid-January did we begin to grieve out loud. The shuttle disaster ran across the nation's television sets, but all we ever saw was little Noah, blurred behind the flood of our tears.

Gracie gathered up our friends and our families and brought them all home to us for the healing. We were blessed beside the river, and slowly. . .our hearts grew wings again.

When a dream lives on in us, it never dies.

"I think it's time to make a baby. What do you think?"

"I think you're on to something, Bunkie."

Several months after we put Noah in the river, we gathered up our familiar dream and made another trip to the clinic. Terryl was so brave to keep trying. It took so much out of us each time we got a negative test result, but how else were we ever going to get a child again?

Noah, are you pulling for us?

So many times I wanted to put blue food coloring into the test just so I could say we were pregnant, but I figured with our luck it would probably make a blue baby. We were not concerned about color, but with two green mothers. . .what would the neighbors think?

"Oh, Honey, it's only our first try since we lost Noah."

"Yes, of course we'll get pregnant."

"No, I don't think there is anything wrong with you."

"Are you kidding? Of course Gracie still hears us. She just told me the other day that if we're going to pursue this, we will need brave, strong hearts. There's the phone. . .I'll get it."

"No, that's okay, Honey; I've got it. Hello. Uh huh. . .what? Yes, of course. Just a minute, let me tell, Judy."

"You are not going to believe this. This is Sarah calling from the hospital. Apparently, there is a baby there who was just born. The mother is from Mexico. She was over here when she started labor, and she wants to adopt out her baby. Do we want it?"

"What? Do you have to ask? Of course!"

"She just got the call from a friend, and she wanted to ask us first. Should I go ahead with this? Okay."

* * *

That baby never made it up the river. Apparently the mother had some trouble communicating what she wanted to a nurse who spoke very little Spanish. Once the social worker got the story clear the following day, the mother had no intention of relinquishing her child for adoption. I began to feel like a ruthless babynapper.

All kinds of strange ideas began to run through my mind. There's a cute one! Should we take him and run? Or, she's a sweetie! You get the car, pull it around to the back of the mall, and I'll nab her. See you in a few minutes! I began to feel like a real ghoul. Of course, the real truth was that we would never want to cause another parent the grief we knew. Better yet, maybe we should make another trip to the clinic.

* * *

"Judy, I'll be forty years old in a few months. Maybe we should go back to Dr. Wyatt and begin the insemination process with you. She thought all along that you'd be a more likely candidate because you're two years younger. What do you say?"

"Our plan was for you to get pregnant first and then me because I have a little more time on my biological clock."

56

"I know, Honey, but in the meantime we've had our first child and lost him and have tried to heal, and I'm not getting any younger."

"Well, how will you feel?"

"I'll watch you grow fat and awkward, and faint during your labor."

* * *

"Hi, Dr. Wyatt. We're back. We tried inseminating Terryl a few times at home using the sperm bank you recommended, but we have not been successful. In the meantime, we adopted a little boy and lost him just before Thanksgiving. Would you be willing to work with us in trying to get me pregnant?"

She was somewhat reserved, but she said she would work with us. We followed all the steps she outlined.

We often felt like chemists during the insemination procedure. Pee in this jar, splash this, swish that, wait . . . now that's something we knew how to do. We decided a person had to be just a little nuts to do it! But nuts or not, we scheduled an appointment with Dr. Wyatt.

"Okay, I'll meet you at the doctor's office. Be sure to be careful driving. Yes, I know it has to travel twenty-five miles while staying frozen so that it doesn't lose its motility, but having you arrive safe with the sample is even more important. See you there."

We met each other at the doctor's office with a brand new set of courage and determination.

"Why is Dr. Wyatt keeping us waiting? She knows we have this time constraint."

"The doctor will see you now."

"Great! Okay, let's go."

"We're waiting in here now. What gives with this doctor?"

"Hello, Dr. Wyatt."

"Hi, um. . . .I've done quite a bit of thinking since you came in last week, and I don't think it's in my best interest or yours to do this insemination. Frankly, the question of lesbian parenting and ethics concerns me. I also do not want to get involved in any litigation concerning this."

"But you said you were comfortable inseminating us just a week ago."

"I know, but I'm just not sure now. And since last week I've been faced with my first lawsuit and. . ."

"I'm sorry to hear that, but we have no reason to want to sue you. Why didn't you tell us you had concerns about our parenting when we came in here before?"

"Okay, I'll do it, since you are here and have the sample. But just this once."

"But will the sample still be any good? We've been waiting now close to an hour."

Dr. Wyatt decided to keep her original agreement with us and inseminate us this one time, but she said she couldn't "take the risk" again.

I laid on the table, my feet in the stirrups, while she performed the insemination. Huge tears welled up inside me. I knew there was no way I could conceive a child in this moment, good sample or not. This was a moment we had waited for with such joy. Would she treat a husband and wife this way? Would they have to leave the office feeling like hungry litigants? We're just women who want desperately to have a baby.

One week after this insemination, we received a check from Dr. Wyatt's office, reimbursing us for the money we had spent. We never went back; we couldn't take the risk again.

It took a couple of months to recover from that experience. We had entrusted ourselves and our dream to another woman, a professional, whom we had contracted with for a service. We had decided to go to a doctor for help because we had tried inseminating on our own a couple of times with no success. We had wanted some professional assistance. We had chosen a woman because we had felt we would have her empathy, if not with our lifestyle, at least with our desire for a child. There were times when recovery seemed distant.

* * *

"What are you looking at, Terryl? What is it?"

She stood at the kitchen counter holding the mail in her hands with a stunned expression on her face.

"It's a note from Barb and Rachel. They sent a picture of Noah."

We stood in a daze and looked at the face of the little boy who had a head of curls, just like Terryl. The back of the picture said "eleven months." We knew. The little boy in the picture was standing inside a crib we did not know. There, attached to the side of the crib, was a little yellow musical duck we had received at our baby shower just a year ago.

"Perfect timing! Don't people know not to call when we can't find the phone for all the tears?"

"Hello. Yes? Oh, hi. You do? Really? When is the baby due? Five months? Well, sure. We haven't turned one down yet."

* * *

Five months later the story ended with another mother changing her mind. We'd been to this river before. Fortunately we'd learned how to use our emotional life preservers and keep enough slack in the rope to get back to shore quickly. But we stayed at the river and kept jumping into those rafts as they came by us. . .we learned that from the children.

Life was such a blend of ups and downs during this time. Grieving is like that. Just when we were standing knee deep in the river, the heavens would open up.

* * *

We found another clinic, and someone who genuinely seemed to want to help us achieve pregnancy. We continued to inseminate, and we began to see a specialist in the seventh month of the process. We both learned more about our bodies than we ever wanted to know. I agreed to a hysterocelpingogram after the eighth insemination. That was an experience! The hospital didn't know what to do with the "other mother" who came with me. By then, we'd learned how to assert ourselves and to push our way through a system otherwise impregnable.

"Just the patient, please. The room is only large enough for you and the doctor."

"If she doesn't go, I don't go."

The test showed that my body was perfectly normal. Two more months. Then a third. Think blue.

"No luck, Honey. It's clear again."

"I can't go through this anymore. This makes eighteen times that you and I together have tried to get pregnant. I have been prayed over. I've shown every part of my body to the world, and so have you. We've used up our friends and our families to cry on and wish with."

We had a positive test one month which dashed its life upon the rocks a week later. We tried four different doctors, including a dear, sweet doctor-friend who prayed with us as he did the insemination. In the meantime, forty began to creep up on me too. Enough.

We could stand on our heads no longer. . .the biological clock was running down. We were getting the message loud and clear now, that despite the difficulties of the adoption system, we must ford the river.

The dream lived on in our hearts.

* * *

There were several more false-alarm adoption calls. We began answering the phone, "Babies R Us!" Didn't we wish.

We decided to call an international adoption agency a friend had mentioned to us just before Noah came into our lives. All of a sudden it felt as though something began to click. . .we could almost hear it!

The preliminary process went smoothly. Within five months we had completed the home study and were approved for an adoption. They told us we would have to wait at least a year. We were experts at that game. After all, this had to be one of the longest labors on record! We were very excited about the international placement, but the thought of another year seemed so very far away. It's hard to stop after chasing a dream for so long. We decided not to let any grass grow under our feet.

Our plan was eventually to adopt a second child, but since we had taken years to come this far and because everything seemed to be going our way, we decided to keep our ears open for another adoption. Because it is not legally possible, at this time, for two lesbians to adopt a child as a couple, we decided to each do paperwork on one of our children, should we be blessed with two.

* * *

"Norma just called. Her mom knows of a woman in Florida who is pregnant with her fifth child and wants to relinquish this one to a home that can provide more than welfare."

"Well, you know our agreement: Any child who wants to come live with us is welcome."

That one took us down some alleys. We hung on a little too long and got some wind knocked out of us. In the end the mother changed her mind.

60

By now we could sure understand it. We wouldn't give up our child either. We did that once, and it's something you never get over.

Gracie, I'm looking for a rainbow.

I'm lookin' with you, Sugar.

There was a child with Down's syndrome who came to our attention. "Yes, we'd love him." The system got hold of him too fast, and two green mothers just wouldn't do.

We have a section in our filing cabinet where we store all the adoptions we've worked on. They document children we held -- some for months, some for days, some just hours — in our prayers and in our minds. "Maybe this one will be ours." There are eleven folders, plus a few other international possibilities and some marked by the caring thoughts of friends. We took each one as far as it would go. And then to the river. . .

There was never a time during the process when we wished we hadn't gone so far. We knew we had gone to that place in the river where the currents and our heartbeat would bring us to that place on the map we'd marked with our dreams so long ago now. But there were many days and many hours when we would look silently at one another and somehow know we were trying to urge the other forward, encourage in the other what we felt might be slipping from ourselves. Following insemination and adoptions not marked with our names took every ounce of energy we had. Faithfully, when the children whom we sought were headed our direction up the river, the waters smoothed and pieces fell into place with ease. That seems to be the way of the river.

Then God said to Noah and to his sons with him, "Behold, I establish my covenant with you and your descendants after you, and with every living creature that is with you, the birds, the cattle, and every beast of the earth with you, as many as came out of the ark. I establish my covenant with you, that never again shall all flesh be cut off by the waters of a flood, and never again shall there be a flood to destroy the earth." And God said, "This is the sign of the covenant which I make between me and you and every living creature that is with you, for all future generations: I set my bow in the cloud, and it shall be a sign of the covenant between me and the earth. When I bring clouds over the earth and the bow is seen in the clouds, I will remember my covenant which is between me and you and every living creature of all flesh; and the waters shall never again become a flood to

destroy all flesh. When the bow is in the clouds, I will look upon it and remember the everlasting covenant between God and every living creature of all flesh that is upon the earth." God said to Noah, "This is the sign of the covenant which I have established between me and all flesh that is upon the earth" (Gen. 9:8-17).

Standing together along the banks of the river, Gracie, Terryl, and I looked skyward for a rainbow.

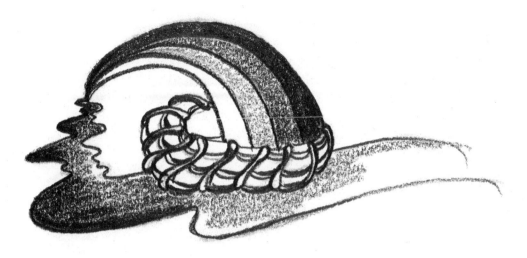

the rainbow

Three years have passed since we lost our Noah. We learned that he is no longer with his birth mother. Just as we expected, the boyfriend left a few weeks after his son arrived home. Susan found she could not juggle school and motherhood. Noah was given to some of her distant relatives less than three months after he was returned to her.

Barb and Rachel are no longer as close to Mrs. Munez, although once in a great while they speak with her. They report to us how Noah is doing and how much bigger he has grown. We don't ask questions about him anymore, and we've not seen another picture.

They sometimes regret having told us about the adoption possibility in the first place. We don't. Had we known that the scenario would have played out the way it did, we may have spared ourselves the ultimate grief, but then we still wouldn't trade our time with Noah for all the books in the library. It is always difficult, but it really is better to have loved and lost than never to have loved at all. In those moments when we feel the loss most deeply, we imagine ourselves having run away with him. We wonder often how we could have played it out to have kept Noah, but it's a life-draining experience to go against the current.

Christmas cards come from Mrs. Munez every year. She "always meant" for us to have him.

* * *

We had been carrying our dreams on the hope of a little girl from a far-off land. It had been close to a year since we had applied when the phone rang one afternoon. It had a familiar ring. It was the pastor of one of my Arizona churches. A young girl in her church was pregnant. Did we want the baby?

"T, she says the birth mom is only fourteen, but she's healthy, and she's due in May."

"May? But our baby girl from overseas should be here around that time."

"I know, and already I have a good feeling about this one. I think this is our other child. We'll raise them together! Let's go with it and trust the river."

"Sounds like an excellent idea to me."

And we were off and rowing.

Every time we hear about another child, we run to the river to check the cargo. Tell me, Gracie, tell me there is no hole in your pocket this time.

Why, Sugar, I've double-stitched the seam in my pocket. This one won't leak out. I've stitched and knit the four of you together. Believe it. Just decide that it's going to be. Just refuse anything else. Just say Yes, and know that I'm right beside you. Seems like sometimes we have to wait for things to ripen before they're ready to drop in our laps. I heard your mother tell you when you were a little girl that "nothing worthwhile comes easy." She waited a long time for you too, and then she got two! You know what they say: All things come to those who wait. Just let yourself believe this, Sugar. They who wait for me "shall renew their strength, they shall mount up with wings like eagles, they shall run and not be weary, they shall walk and not faint" [Isa. 40:31]. So let's fly on down to the river, Sugar.

We scheduled a meeting with the pending Grandmother at a conference just a month after the original call came. We had learned not to get crazed with the first sighting of a floating basket. Because this baby was not due for seven months, we decided to ease into it.

Our first meeting went very well. We were actually rather willing to trust the river at this point because we had just been approved for our second international adoption. Even though that would bring us the two children we wanted, we had never yet turned down the possibility of a child coming to live with us, and we decided to carry this through to see where it would lead.

We were very aware of the similarities between this adoption and the one with Noah. We were certainly aware of the risks involved. Still we felt strongly that we should pursue it.

We said we might consider another independent adoption if we found a baby in a basket with final papers on our doorstep. We had certainly experienced the worst possible scenario, but we didn't want to turn away from any possibility. Independent adoptions are tough to accomplish. When you deal openly with the birth mother, you lay yourself wide open. And if you lose, you lose twice. You lose your child, and the relationship with the birth mother is broken in the midst of a shattered dream. The legal hassles, the costs incurred to care for the birth mother during her pregnancy and the counseling that she will most likely need can add up immensely. . .especially the second time around. The emotional pressures welling up and up become intense, and we knew we would have to prepare ourselves for the rapids once again. Yet once a dream is planted deep within your heart, it does not uproot easily. We wanted to be sure that we didn't let a child pass us by in the river if this just might be the one coming with our names written on its heart.

We arranged to meet the birth mother the following month when I visited one of the churches in my district. When we arrived, we spotted a young girl standing at the door who looked ever so faintly as if she might be carrying a child.

"She's so young. She's just a little girl. Isn't she a doll! Do you think this is going to work?"

"That, my friend, is the question of our lives! And the answer? Bingo. Yes, of course! I'll chat with her a little tonight while you mingle with the church people. I have a very good sense about this."

"That, my dear heart, is music to my ears. What time should I tell them to come to the hotel for our meeting tomorrow?"

"Four o'clock sounds great."

* * *

"I'm a nervous wreck. All of this is just too deja vu for me. I mean, are we sure we want to get into this place again? I know but. . .Yes, but. . .Okay, so I'm a coward. It's tough living with Queen Lancelot."

"Very funny, Darling."

"Thank you. They're here, there's the little rap on the castle door. I shall get it, Your Highness. Give me a smooch for the road, Bunkie."

"Hi! Sure, come in. No, no, you're right on time. We were just finishing up. Come in, sit down."

Here we are, Gracie. There's a baby in this room. The baby is in repose right now, but I can almost see it through her tummy. Don't let me stare. I feel like a three-year-old.

You're acting like one! Relax, Sugar.

Our meeting with the birth mother was wonderful. We all shared what we thought and how we felt. We laughed and cried and found ourselves loving a little fourteen-year-old girl whom we found waiting beside the river. The characters were different, but the story looked and felt very similar to our original meeting with Noah's mother. We knew what we were going to do. We would just sit and watch the movie to the end. Not all stories end the same.

* * *

The following morning I was scheduled to preach in the church where I was visiting. As I approached the pulpit, I was taken back to the first time I saw another woman moving to the same space. Her river story now roared in my ears and standing there among the people whom I had come to know and love, I saw a panoramic view through a familiar window.

It was as though the focus ring on my camera had just adjusted itself to the clearest vision I had ever seen.

I watched myself walking into that Metropolitan Community Church thirteen years earlier. I greeted a woman in the pulpit and followed her to the river. Not long after I met Gracie, standing there in the midst of my people, loving us all in her warm, untiring arms. Then Terryl joined us. . .and later Noah. And then we took him to the river. I felt all those old feelings of waiting and longing which accompanied the many inseminations and the many false adoption starts. I rolled over again in my mind the conversations I'd had with my mother about insemination and her fear that I was somehow stepping outside the will of God. I saw how my trip through the church was a continual coming to realize how we must speak our dreams boldly and clearly and not give up. I heard again the debates about "artificial reproduction," "illegitimate children," "adopted kids with no roots." Simultaneously I heard Gracie straining to awaken us all from such strange notions. Illegitimate children?

Remember how my boy child came to live with you. . . illegitimate by your standards today. He had no birth father to live with him. Adopted children? Well, those children are my eagles. While you're looking for their roots, remember. . . I give them wings! Children — whether they are adopted or born into a two-parent family or a single-parent family or a two-mother family, from a test tube or a donor — are each one of my miracles.

Gracie, I sure wish other people could hear you sometimes!

We will no doubt always wonder a little why neither of us was able to bear children, but here, in this panoramic view, I saw two children moving closer to our home, one from a far off land and the other from my home state, and out of the church family where it all began. Gracie was knitting us together like the wonderful story of another expectant family we were hearing from the pulpit, as I left this vision in my mind and was drawn back to the moment. . .

. . .you will find a babe wrapped in swaddling cloths. . . . (Luke 2:12).

I looked out into the congregation and saw a little fourteen-year-old girl — a child with a baby — sitting next to her mother and Terryl. I looked around the church, watching the Christmas tree lights blur a little through a mist in my eyes. Maybe there will be Christmas again after all.

Merry Christmas, Sugar.

* * *

We left that young Arizona mother, believing very strongly in our hearts that we would return someday soon to bring our child home. Our drive back was filled with delight. The desert is a wonderful place for happiness.

Shortly after returning home from Arizona, we received our call from the international adoption agency.

"YOOOOOOOEEEEEUUUU!!!!*****!!!!!"

"YEAHHHHHHHH!!!!!!! Hot dogs. . .pickles. . .give me pickles! Boil water! Yeah, thank you, thank you, thank you, yeah, yeah!"

"Bunkie doo dah, Bunkie yeah, my oh my, what a wonderful day. Our baby has been born, oi vey!"

We danced around our kitchen like two silly mothers. And for the first time in years. . .we were.

"Can you believe this? Ha! Two at a time! This gives a whole new meaning to the words 'when it rains it pours.' Jordan has been born. Our little Jordan has been born!"

"Jordan. What do you think about the name? Is it the right one?"

We held each other for a silent moment and stopped to gather our joy. "When it rains, it pours . . ."

"Are we ever going to have to put her in the river? Oh please, tell me no."

"No, we won't ever have to put her in the river."

There was a huge smile that swept over our hearts in the moment of that question.

"No, we will never have to give her to the river because she is the river."

"What?"

"Jordan. The River Jordan. She is the river. That's her name. . .what a great name!"

"Oh my God, dearest Gracie, why didn't you ever let me think of that."

I knew you'd catch on. Besides, Sugar, you're responsible for what you think. I only get to squeeze a word in edgewise from time to time. By the way, little Jordan is a beauty.

Of course she is. She's one of yours.

The next several weeks were spent waiting at the mailbox. The paper-work was stuck in the Christmas mail, and we didn't get the picture of Jordan for almost six weeks. Christmas was filled with friends and spoiling each other rotten.

"This is our last Christmas without children. Let's make each other sick with presents."

Some friends of ours who lost a child from a miscarriage around the same time we lost Noah finally got their little girl from Mexico. We had Christmas dinner with them and "gooooed" together at the table. Friends and family were close.

To help fill the time while we awaited our picture of Jordan and the birth of our Arizona baby, I cleaned out the garage and decided to unpack the bassinet, car seat, odds and ends we'd saved from Noah. I brushed the two-and-a-half years of dust off of everything and brought it inside. Time to set this up by the river. I had the bassinet set up when Terryl came home from work one evening.

"Oh, Judy, that looks so sweet. It's kind of hard seeing it though, isn't it?"

"Yeah . . ."

"Can we go through his things together tonight?"

Next to the bassinet was the kite we had made for Noah in Sausalito the day he was born. And a box with all the little outfits people had sent from around the country. And the blanket I knitted him . . .

"Oh, Judy . . ."

Terryl held up two little hangers with the name NOAH painted on them. "Oh, it's okay, but it's so hard. We should have sent these with him. No, that's right, she didn't call him Noah."

We went through the rest of his little hope chest and wove our way in and out of the remnants of our grief.

We send you our love, little Noah. We long for the day we will see you again . . . somewhere over the rainbow.

* * *

Jordan's picture finally arrived. She is a beauty. She looks just like Gracie! We're not surprised.

They tell us at the adoption agency that when she arrives, we will be met by her escorts who will have her in a "Moses basket." She should arrive any day.

We received one more possible adoption call just minutes after Jordan's picture arrived. It always seemed to work that way. For the very first time we said No. We knew our family was almost home.

Well, Sugar, you and your Terryl are almost to the river. Remember, in my pocket there is always a blessing. You'll be needing some with two children. Sometimes when I look out there at my family, my pride just swells with delight that you all have faith so big and pretty. All those folks around you over the past few years, just loving you both. And your love for each other looks real nice, real nice. Look, Sugar . . . there's a rainbow up ahead.

"What are you doing, Honey?"

"Waiting at the river. Look, here comes a Moses basket!"

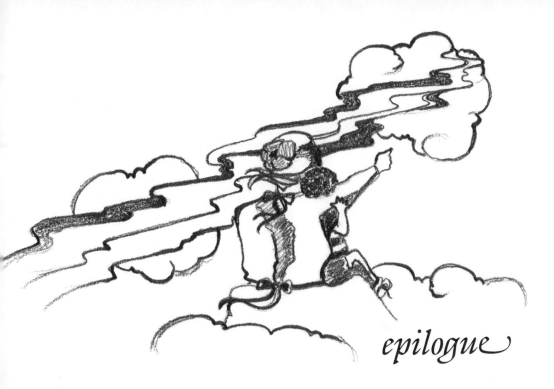

epilogue

Judy and Terryl stood beside the river for a very long time. From the first day they talked about children, they kept their hope alive. I watched them throughout their journey and was so taken by them as they prepared for the homecoming of their children. First they prepared for Jordan. They had only a few days' notice of her arrival.

The call came on a Friday morning. Judy's hands were shaking so much it took three or four dialings for her to get through to Terryl at work. Terryl came home, and they left for a weekend away before Jordan would arrive Sunday afternoon. Their weekend was filled with wonderings. . .they talked endlessly of their new little baby daughter.

It was quite a scene at the airport that Sunday afternoon. They brought two friends along to take pictures. I engraved the picture in my mind. How amazing it was for me to watch these two finally realizing their dream. They stood in the midst of the boarding area, mostly unaware of the people who surrounded them, people from every walk of life, waiting for family and friends to arrive. They stood off to one side, trying to be as inconspicuous as possible but somehow standing out in the crowd. It's hard to shade the glow from the pot at the end of the rainbow. . .and they had finally arrived. The plane landed and their hearts took flight. They hugged one another close until the plane came to the gate. The first person *off the plane was a flight attendant carrying a Moses basket. She walked down the stairs and put the basket on the ramp. Judy said "That's our baby!" loud enough for the airline employee to hear, so she smiled and hollered back over the roar of the engines, "She's on her way out!"*

The entire plane unloaded before the escort descended the stairs with a tiny little bundle. Terryl and Judy had waited with what no doubt felt like contractions to them, each person coming from the plane like a wave of labor which pushed out from inside them until "There, oh there, there's our little darling!"

The escort had no difficulty knowing who this bundle belonged to. Judy and Terryl stood like proud expectant parents. They had been crying for the past ten minutes, and yet they smiled and hugged until they reached out for their little girl. It was a silent, sacred moment as the escort handed Jordan to them. They looked down into the receiving blanket and saw a very small, beautifully brown little girl who had eyes with pictures of them written inside. Her eyes were clear and soft and sleepy. She was very weak, and she made no noise, but she had the soul of an angel. They knew for sure that their little girl had finally come home to them.

They thanked the escort with gifts and a hug, and then they turned their backs on a very long, very difficult journey as the three of them together, arm-in-arm, in arms, turned their sweet, sacred faces on a new life.

* * *

Jordan arrived with a cold. She weighed just a little over seven pounds at four and a half months. At birth she had been only slightly over two pounds. She had spent those first months being well cared for and nurtured in a hospital for abandoned children. She was very tiny and weak. That first night was an incredible experience for her new moms. I watched from a corner in their hearts as they whispered around her about her wonder and her beauty. She really is a beauty, if I do say so myself! They were so gentle and tender with her and so careful to listen to her needs and to begin to know her. They cried off and on, quiet tears that often come from my people at the end of an answered dream. I catch those tears and store them up for holy water. They called their families and some of them cried too. . .they had often wondered and worried what would happen if this day did not come for Judy and Terryl. They called a few friends. All of them together painted a new little circle of stars in the sky with their joy that holy night. I called off the shepherds and kings, but I did send an angel.

Just before Judy and Terryl decided to sleep, Terryl said, "Look at Jordan, Honey. It looks like she's talking to someone. Watch her mouth. . ."

"Hmmm, I see what you mean. Wonder what she's doing?"

"I think she's talking to her guardian angel; no doubt she's had one these past four and a half months. . ."

I was glad they recognized the gift.

The next day they took Jordan to a pediatrician. She was anemic, congested, and showed very poor muscle tone. The doctor encouraged them to take her to a developmental specialist, once she was settled and they'd had more time alone with her. It was frightening for them to think that Jordan may have come with some developmental problems, but their joy was undaunted. They began to work with her and exercise her muscles. She improved steadily. By the time they got to their appointment with the specialist, they were told she was perfect.

People had held off on giving showers this time until after Jordan arrived. It did my heart so much good to see people welcoming their little girl and opening to their joy as much as they did. Her little nursery filled up with bears and rabbits and dresses and Oshkosh! They had hung the kite made for Noah over her crib. Jordan spent hours looking at the porpoise and the long lavendar, pink, and blue tail which draped over her. She would know the boy who could have been her brother in some ways. They had saved that kite in the garage all that time and now it hung with memories of a little boy and hung so sweetly for their little girl. They smiled remembering. Someday they will tell Jordan about Noah. . .maybe as they fly the kite on some wonderfully sunny, bright afternoon. If I were you, I'd be looking for a kite with a porpoise and a very happy family below.

Judy made the crib quilt for Jordan, a pink and purple penguin. Her nursery was such a fun place for my angel. She came home once to tell me what a treat it was to be living in a home with so much love. She told me she'd never had such a nice job. So I've let her stay on. Gifts and flowers flooded the place for weeks. It was great!

They are truly blessed with this child. They know it too. Every night as they hold Jordan before putting her into her crib, they say a prayer to her guardian angel. Terry's grandmother used to say it with her when she was a little girl, and it has become part of their nightly ritual. Jordan is one of the happiest babies on earth. She smiles and giggles and grows with such grace. . .hmmm.

The entire time Jordan was settling into her new home with her new parents, the birth mother for the Tucson baby was calling every week. It felt almost unbelievable and a little scary to them that they could possibly have another child in their home in less than four months after the arrival of Jordan. But the birth mother never wavered. They spoke freely and openly with each other about their fears and joy and excitement all along. They were feeling selfish about wanting more time with Jordan before another child came to live with them, but they knew that if this was their other little child, they wanted the baby to come to their home and find all the doors open. They began to talk with Jordan about her little brother or sister. The three of them together continued to dogear the baby name books. Jordan chewed on them, and Terry and Judy laughed at how long this process had gone on.

In the eighth month of pregnancy the birth mother spoke with the expectant family every week, and the last week they spoke every day. The doctor felt sure she would be late in delivering this child. They held their hearts close over those last few days. They walked toward the moment with their hearts replaying the last few days before Noah's delivery. They felt somewhat different in that thay had a little girl whom they loved and cherished, and yet this second child had grown, like Jordan, in their dreams and had become an important part of their family and their lives already. They could see so many similarities to Noah's birth each step of the way, and yet their connection to the birth mother had never been anything but good. The birth mother even called to ask them what names they had come up with so that she could put that on the birth certificate. She had invited them into the delivery room for the actual birth, and she said all along she knew she was doing the right thing for herself and her child.

The guardian angel who worked for me in their home awakened me at a rude hour to tell me Judy and Terry had just received the call from the intermediary. "We're in labor." Again labor had begun at 1:30 in the morning. They shared a few bits of information on the phone. Then Judy and Terryl packed and prepared for departure. They got the car all ready

74

and then went up to get their little girl. As always, Jori awoke with a sweet smile and hugs to share. The three of them took off to find the baby they had all been waiting for. My angel had to hurry out the door with them to make the trip across the desert.

They stopped for gas and coffee and asked me to keep them safe. . .gladly!

They still had not decided on a name, so they did names for the first three hours of the trip while Jori slept and occasionally blessed them with a grin from the back seat.

I was eager for them to stop for breakfast so they could call the hospital and get an update. When they did, they learned that their baby boy had been born. The birth mother and their son were fine. The labor was short — only three and a half hours — but he got hung up in the birth canal and they had to do a forceps delivery. He had very fair skin, deep blue eyes, and light brown hair. He weighed in at seven pounds, two and a half ounces, and was twenty inches long. A fine dream come true. They were thrilled and yet sad to have missed the delivery.

I reminisced about the day my son was born. I remember the thrill, the expectation, the concern, the unspoken worry, the spoken joy. I wanted to send them another angel for this weary family, traveling with little sleep across the desert in the wee hours of the morning. I sent them an angel with a laugh, and that laugh today lives inside little Andrew Tyler. They had finally landed on a name!

Seeing him for the first time in the hospital was an awesome experience. The hospital was prepared to make them feel welcome and special. The nurses were kind, warm, thrilled with and for them. They went into the nursery together, and a nurse held their little boy up to them with a grin. They had left Jori with Judy's niece in town so that they could have these first few precious moments to share alone with their son — though they did wish Jori were there to meet her new little brother.

They were quiet with him, and they called me into the moment. I went with such joy; I was thrilled for them. They had no words. I knew they carried some fear about a possible loss, but they had stopped to see the sweet little birth mother before going to see Andrew, and she was still resolved. They began to trust their new love for this long-awaited son.

I sat beside them as they looked and shared those first tender moments *with Andy. It did my heart so much good. They have made a new story for me to write in the book of life. I am proud to be their amazing mother, friend, sister, grandmother, Gracie!*

* * *

Today they live beside the river with their children. They speak to the children of dreaming and believing, and they tell them every day that dreams do come true! They are a family made from dreaming, and it shows.

...and they came into the ark two by two...

Author
Judy Dahl

Searching out her spiritual roots has been at the heart of Judy's life. Born and raised in Phoenix, Arizona, she attended Roman Catholic schools for twelve years. Shortly after high school, she entered a Benedictine convent in Duluth, Minnesota. After graduating summa cum laude from Metropolitan State College in Denver, Colorado with a degree in human services, Judy completed her masters of divinity from the Iliff School of Theology in Denver, Colorado.

Judy now serves as an ordained minister in the Universal Fellowship of Metropolitan Community Churches and is the District Coordinator for the southwestern region.

Along with her life's work, Judy finds deep fulfillment in "making home." She is a gourmet cook who also loves to sew, garden, to do interior design and photography, and create stained glass art. Placing great value on friendships and family, Terryl and Judy have found a still greater treasure with the arrival of their two children. Judy lives in Laguna Niguel, California where her dream for family has found a home and her spiritual search continues.

Artist
Carol Jeanotilla

A fine artist most of her life, Carol spent eighteen years in a nursing career before being catapulted back to design school during a mid-life crisis. She graduated with honors in March 1987 from the Colorado Institute of Art.

Carol is now a designer and the Art Director for Unison Marketing and Communications, an advertising agency specializing in healthcare clients. She also freelances design, illustration, and packaging from her Aurora, Colorado studio. Her special talent is visual interpretation of the written word.

Carol was born in Indiana, grew up in Delaware, spent a stint in Maine, and now gratefully calls Colorado home. Eight of her twelve years in Colorado have been spent lovingly with her partner, Kathryn. After several years as "mountain women," the pair now is carrying out long-range career goals. Carol and her sixteen-year-old son, Eric, a budding writer, hope to collaborate on a book someday.

the
WOMEN'S
series

LURAMEDIA presents

The hallmark of The Women's Series is honest and lively writing that articulates the full range of women's experiences. Our dream is to publish short books or tapes in many forms — poetry, dialogues, monologues, journaling excerpts, personal stories, letters — that will speak woman-to-woman across space and time. We want women to hear these voices, feel comforted and challenged, because they, too, have felt the same emotions and seen the same visions.

THE WOMEN'S SERIES includes...
Superwoman Turns 40 by Donna Schaper
   The story of one woman's intentions to grow up. For women turning around in the middle of life and coming home to themselves. Celebrate the small gifts of caring in the midst of life's chaotic demands.
   (ISBN 0-931055-67-1)

River of Promise by Judy Dahl
   An unusual story of love and adoption. For all those engaged in the struggles and joys of raising children in a nontraditional family. Speaks with warmth and compassion to the issue of adoption by single and homosexual parents.
   (ISBN 0-931055-64-4)

Circle of Stones by Judith Duerk (due August 1988)
   A collection of reflections, imagery, and stories for women who are rediscovering their identity. Emphasizes the importance of letting one's unique spirit come to birth and attending to the inner voice.
   (ISBN 0-931055-66-0)

To Love Delilah by Mary Cartledge-Hayes (due October 1988)
   Through fiction, poetry, essays, and journaling suggestions, Delilah and other "wicked women" in the Bible are separated from the negative myths surrounding them. The reader moves to a new understanding of the biblical women and of themselves.
   (ISBN 0-931055-68-7)

LuraMedia PUBLICATIONS

by Marjory Zoet Bankson
BRAIDED STREAMS
Esther and a Woman's Way
of Growing
(ISBN 0-931055-05-09)

SEASONS OF FRIENDSHIP
Naomi and Ruth
as a Pattern
(ISBN 0-931055-41-5)

by Alla Renee Bozarth
WOMANPRIEST
A Personal Odyssey
(ISBN 0-931055-51-2)

by Lura Jane Geiger
ASTONISH ME, YAHWEH!
Leader's Guide
(ISBN 0-931055-02-4)

by Lura Jane Geiger
and Patricia Backman
BRAIDED STREAMS
Leader's Guide
(ISBN 0-931055-09-1)

by Lura Jane Geiger, Sandy Landstedt,
Mary Geckeler, and Peggy Oury
ASTONISH ME, YAHWEH!
A Bible Workbook-Journal
(ISBN 0-931055-01-6)

by Kenneth L. Gibble
THE GROACHER FILE
A Satirical Expose of
Detours to Faith
(ISBN 0-931055-55-5)

by Ronna Fay Jevne, Ph.D.
and Alexander Levitan, M.D.
NO TIME FOR NONSENSE
Self-Help for the Seriously Ill
(ISBN 0-931055-63-6)

by Ted Loder
EAVESDROPPING ON THE ECHOES
Voices from the Old Testament
(ISBN 0-931055-42-3)

GUERRILLAS OF GRACE
Prayers for the Battle
(ISBN 0-931055-01-6)

NO ONE BUT US
Personal Reflections on
Public Sanctuary
(ISBN 0-931055-08-3)

TRACKS IN THE STRAW
Tales Spun from the Manger
(ISBN 0-931055-06-7)

by Jacqueline McMakin
with Sonya Dyer
WORKING FROM THE HEART
For Those Who Hunger for Meaning
and Satisfaction in Their Work
(ISBN 0-931055-65-2)

by Elizabeth O'Connor
SEARCH FOR SILENCE
Revised Edition
(ISBN 0-931055-07-5)

by Renita Weems
JUST A SISTER AWAY
A Womanist Vision of Women's
Relationships in the Bible
(ISBN 0-931055-52-0)

LuraMedia is a company that searches for ways to encourage personal
growth, shares the excitement of creative integrity, and believes in the
power of faith to change lives.